DATE DUE
GAYLORD
PRINTED IN U.S.A.
D0931271
By AUTH
By the AMERIC
At the THEATRE in Williamsburg, this
An English Comick
LOVE in a
Justice WOODCOCK by
HAWTHORN by
Young MEADOWS
Sir WILLIAM MEAD
Servants at the Statute by Mr. GOO
Mr. ROBERTS, Mrs. HENRY,
Mrs. TOMLINSON, Miss RIC
The ORCHESTRA to be
To which will be adde
The B U
The ENGLISH
The BUCK by
Mr. SUBTLE by
CLASSICK
SOLITAIRE
MARQUIS by
Sir JOHN BUCK by Mr. ROBER
DAUPHINE by Mr. ROBER
Mrs. SUBTLE by Miss RICHAR
LUCINDA (with a SONG) by Miss
BY PERMISSION
Worshipful the MAYOR of WILLIAMSBURG
the BENEFIT of Mrs. PARKER)
At the old THEATRE, near the CAPITOL,
COMPANY of COMEDIANS, on FRIDAY the 3d of JUNE,
will be presented
Beggar's Opera.
Macheath, by Mr. VERLING.
(Being his first Appearance in that Character)
Mr. CHARLTON.
Mr. FARRELL.
Mr. PARKER.
Mr. WALKER.
Mr. BROMADGE.
Mr. MALLORY.
Mr. GODWIN.
and LUCY LOCKIT, by Mrs. OSBORNE.
Miss DOWTHAITT.
Miss YAPP.
Mrs. DOWTHAITT.
Mr. WALKER.
ANA TRAPES, by Mr. PARKER.
Peachum, by Mrs. PARKER.
GODWIN will perform the DANCE called
The DRUNKEN PEASANT.
PEASANT, CLOWN, by Mr. GODWIN. Mr. PARKER.
To which will be added a FARCE, called
The ANATOMIST,
OR
Sham Doctor.
Le MEDICIN (the French Doctor) by Mr. GODWIN.
Old GERALD, Young GERALD, CRISPIN, MARTIN, SIMON BURLEY, by Mr. PARKER. Mr. CHARLTON. Mr. VERLING. Mr. FARRELL. Mr. WALKER.
ANGELICA, DOCTOR's WIFE, WAITING WOMAN, by Miss YAPP, Mrs. DOWTHAITT. Miss DOWTHAITT.
BEATRICE, by Mrs. PARKER.
The MUSICK of the OPERA will be conducted by Mr. PELHAM,
BY AUTH
By the AMERICA
At the THEATRE in WILLIAMSBURG, this present WEDNESDAY
(the 20th of JUNE)
The Clandestine Marriage.
Lord OGLEBY by Mr. HALLAM.
Sir JOHN MELVIL by Mr BYERLEY.
LOVEWELL by Mr. PARKER.
STERLING by Mr. MORRIS.
Serjeant FLOWER by Mr. DOUGLASS.
BRUSH by Mr. HENRY.
CANTON by Mr. HARMAN.
TRAVERSE by Mr. ROBERTS.
TRUMAN by Mr. WOOLLS.
Mrs. HEIDELBERG by Mrs. DOUGLASS.
FANNY by Miss RICHARDSON.
BETTY by Mrs. HENRY.
CHAMBERMAID by Mrs. HALLAM.
Miss STERLING by Miss HALLAM.
To which will be added a MUSICAL ENTERTAINMENT, called
HOMAS & SALLY:
Or, The Sailor's Return.
The SQUIRE by Mr. WOOLLS.
The SAILOR by Mr. HENRY.
DORCAS by Mrs HARMAN.
SALLY by Miss HALLAM.
Doors will be opened at 6, and the Play begin precisely at 7 o'Clock.
TS to be had at the POST OFFICE, of Mr. PATRICK GALT
and of Mr. JAMES RUSSELL, at
6d. PIT and GALLERY
Jeremie, Diggory, And Tony Lumpkin, (with a song)
Mrs. Hardcastle, Miss Neville, Penelope, And Miss Hardcastle,
EDGAR. WATTS. KEDEY.
Mr. EVANS. Mr. FURNELL. Mr. BIGNALL.
BETWEEN PLAY AND FARCE,
A Favorite Song, by Mrs.
Four and Twenty Fiddlers, (a comic song) by Mr. Watts.
A SONG, by Mrs.
Honest Bob of the Mill, (a comic song) by Mr. Bignall.
To which will be added the favorite Farce, of
All the World's a Stag
OR,
The Butler in Buskins.
Charles Stanley, Simon, Diggory, (the Butler) And Sir Gilbert Pumpkin,
Mr. KEDEY. Mr. EDGAR. Mr. EVANS. Mr. BIGNAL Mr. WATTS.
Miss Kitty Sprightly, And Miss Bridget Pumpkin,
Tickets—at one dollar each, to be had at the different Taverns and of
E Copeland's.
No admittance behind the Scenes.
To-Morrow—The Tragedy of Douglass, with the Farce of Miss in her
On Friday—The Contrast, or American Son of Liberty, with the Farce of
On Saturday—The Provok'd Husband, with the Farce of The Deuce is

SONGS FROM THE WILLIAMSBURG THEATRE

SONGS FROM THE WILLIAMSBURG THEATRE

A Selection of Fifty Songs Performed on the Stage in Williamsburg in the Eighteenth Century

Arranged for
Voice and Keyboard and with Introduction and Historical Commentaries
by
JOHN W. MOLNAR

Foreword by
CARLETON SPRAGUE SMITH

THE COLONIAL WILLIAMSBURG FOUNDATION
WILLIAMSBURG, VIRGINIA
Distributed by the University Press of Virginia,
Charlottesville, Virginia

Library of Congress Catalog Card No. 78–165363
Colonial Williamsburg ISBN: 0–910412–86–3
University Press of Virginia ISBN: 0–8139–0381–5

Printed in the United States of America

Table of Contents

Foreword

THERE can be no question that colonial Virginians were thoroughly familiar with songs of the theatre. Many of them collected plays, scores, books, and critical essays about music and drama, especially English lyric drama, whose most characteristic form consisted of plays with interspersed music. When the tunes were essential to the text the composite was known as "ballad opera" or "English opera."

Spoken dialogue, punctuated by intelligible songs in the vernacular, has long had an immediate appeal to Anglo-Saxons. This sort of music, simple and easy to follow, containing plots dealing with everyday subjects—social, political, or patriotic—instantly makes its point.

We must remember that the lyric theatre provided an opportunity for sociable gatherings, and the audience expected to be entertained. Witty and satirical dialogue combined with melodious songs and gay dances, which amateurs as well as professionals could and frequently did perform, made attending plays with music a delightful experience.

During the eighteenth century, professionals became more and more important in colonial theatre music, yet they had a close relationship with amateurs. The extent to which the latter made music is apt to be forgotten in this mechanical age.

During the 1730s and 1740s Virginians avidly read Fielding, Garrick, and Richardson, and the music of Henry Purcell, Handel, Boyce, Arne, and even Vivaldi was played by amateurs and professionals alike. A mid-century letter reads: "Scarce an Evening (as Dicky can tell you) but we are entertain'd with the performance of Felton's, Handel's and Vivally's [*sic*] compositions."

Philip Fithian, tutor to the children of Councilor Robert Carter of Nomini Hall in the 1770s, relates that his employer owned many instruments and played on them frequently and with great skill. And Thomas Jefferson, an accomplished violinist, owned *The Beggar's Opera*, *Thomas and Sally*, *Artaxerxes*, *Love in a Village*, and *The Padlock*—as well as a two-volume London collection of drinking songs.

Jefferson even had the Italian musician Francesco Alberti as a music master in residence at Monticello. "Alberti came over with a troop of players and afterwards taught music in Williamsburg," he told Nicholas Trist. "Subsequently I got him to come up here [Monticello] and took lessons for several years. I suppose that during at least a dozen years of my life, I played no less than *three hours* a day."

When we read of plays performed by "the young Gentlemen and Ladies of the Country," or of "a Set of Private Gentlemen providing the Instrumental Musick of each Air," or realize the numerous plays and quantities of music to be found in colonial libraries, it becomes obvious to us that amateurs devoted more time to singing and playing than do their descendants today.

In short, music and drama did not take second place behind the other arts in Williamsburg. Organ recitals were given in Bruton Parish Church, thanks to Peter Pelham, the church's first organist. The most fashionable entertainment, of course, was found at the playhouse, and there the inhabitants of the capital and visitors to it enjoyed the same theatre music as that heard in Great Britain.

* * *

Professor Molnar's detailed and handsome collection of theatre songs performed in and associated with Williamsburg is a milestone on the important sea road between Great Britain and the Old Dominion, and of value both to the general reader and to students of American civilization. Scholars will greet this publication enthusiastically, for such documentation on songs popular in the colonies has never been gathered before. The historical commentaries are rich with information, and the notes are treated with a thoroughness and authority that are most welcome.

This is an outstanding contribution to our knowledge of the performing arts in the colonial era, and from now on anyone curious to know about the theatre and music of the period must consult this work. It should be on the shelves of every library, public and private, that prides itself on containing the musical and social history of our country.

CARLETON SPRAGUE SMITH

Preface

THE playgoers of colonial Virginia heard most if not all of the songs in this book performed in Williamsburg's eighteenth-century theatres. Undoubtedly they also played and sang them in their homes for their own enjoyment.

In the repertoires of the various theatrical companies that played on the Williamsburg stage, some hundred-odd plays, ballad operas, and comic operas can be counted. Very likely there was music in most of them. I have been able to identify about two hundred songs that were performed during the action or between the acts of above eighty of these vehicles. From those two hundred I have selected the fifty you find here.

A number of factors governed the selection. In the first place, I limited the choice to songs that were performed in plays presented—by documentary proof or virtual certainty—in the Virginia capital. Two exceptions are "Wher' did you borrow that last Sigh?" selected because of its connection with Governor Sir William Berkeley, and "Water parted from the Sea," which was so often heard as an inter-act and concert song and so often performed by Virginians that it could not be overlooked.

Other factors included the songs' historical and present-day interest, their musical worth, vitality and appeal, and the desire to include a variety of musical styles. I further refined the selection by including songs representative of those sung in the different types of plays that were offered to the Williamsburg public. Some were chosen because their words or music, or both, were used in more than one play. A number were reluctantly dropped because, although they were sung on the colonial circuit, documentation of their performance in Williamsburg is not as firm as it is for those that are included.

The final consideration in the choice of the songs was the availability of the music, as only the first or the earliest appropriate obtainable edition of each song was used as the source. Many of them were readily accessible in the collection at the Research Department of Colonial Williamsburg and in the play collection at the Earl Gregg Swem Library of the College of William and Mary. Others were secured from holdings in England, Scotland, and elsewhere in the United States.

Specific guides were kept in mind in arranging the songs. Whenever an orchestra score had been printed and was available, as indicated with those songs, I made a keyboard reduction. When the bass of the song (i.e., the foundation of the harmonic structure) was printed with the melody (indicated by "bass given"), I harmonized the song in conformity with it. In those instances in which only the melody of the song was printed (indicated by "melody only"), I supplied the harmonization.

I attempted to make the arrangements rather simple and straightforward, and of interest not only to the singer but to the pianist playing them alone, to the casual amateur performer as well as to one interested in the eighteenth-century theatre in all its ramifications. I tried to keep the flavor if not the substance of the typical part played by the harpsichordist in a small provincial theatre of the time. He would have been called on to sustain and help the singer by playing the melody almost continuously, even as do theatre orchestras of today in the typical musical-comedy orchestration. He would also have had to play the all-important bass line, filling in the middle harmonies as best he could, depending on his skill at realization (i.e., supplying the harmonization from the bass) and ability at the keyboard. Exceptions to this type of arrangement are the piano reductions of full scores.

I made no attempt to "over-realize" (i.e., over-elaborate or over-embellish) the accompaniment. Of course, in a concert performance, a more free, improvisational style, in keeping with the harmonic structure, with less doubling of the voice part, would be appropriate and stylistically correct. I left the bass figuration in all scores in which it was given.

The word "song" as used in the commentaries generally implies both words and music. According to definition, "song" may mean not only the music but a poem written usually to be set to music. The latter usage especially by nineteenth- and twentieth-century writers of works on ballads and poetry has sometimes led to confusion, the authors of the verses being mistaken for the composers. Because new words were written for familiar tunes, and new tunes provided for older verses, the necessary distinction was made in the commentaries by using "air," "music," "melody," or "tune" for the music, "song text" or "verse text" for the words, or by stating that the author wrote the song and the musician composed the setting for it.

I found the music of the songs in various sources. Sometimes the printed play texts included the tunes, the "Musick prefix'd" to the plays; this was especially true of the ballad operas. Some instances printed only the name of a tune above the song text; others used (as title) the first line of an earlier song to identify the air to which the words were to be sung.

Printed play texts, particularly of mainpieces, more often included only the verses of a song without any musical indication; in some cases there appeared merely the designation "A Song." The identity of some of these I traced in biographical and critical studies of the playwrights and plays. By searching catalogues of library holdings, in particular the *British Union-Catalogue* edited by Edith Schnapper, I could locate the song—either in single-sheet form or in a collection or in a periodical. I was then able, by photocopy, to obtain the earliest appropriate edition; the source notations for the music as well as the bibliography, indicate the depositories that sent copies.

Many of the songs were headed "Sung by [name of the performer] in [name of the play]." Not only does this information place the song in that play, but it also indicates the popularity of both the song and the singer, as well as helping to date the first performance of that edition of the song.

The Earl Gregg Swem Library of the College of William and Mary possesses a large collection of first and early editions of the plays. These were the principal source of the play texts. My wife read all the plays in order to secure the background for the portions of the commentaries that deal with the plots of the plays. In those cases where there were a number of editions, all available were checked to make sure that the song was retained over the period of years in which the colonial theatre was in existence. In those instances in which a song was interpolated into a play, it was necessary to find the most likely place wherein the song was sung.

In the commentaries the term "singer and actor" refers to one featured as a singer in the theatre bills and concerts, and "singing actor" to an actor cast in roles that required singing.

Since by 1763 the successor company to the Hallams was known variously as "Mr. Douglass and his Company of Comedians" and the "American Company of Comedians," the latter name is used in the commentaries in order to avoid confusion.

ACKNOWLEDGMENTS

I would like to express my thanks to all who sent me copies of music or permitted me to see collections. These were: Mr. A. Hyatt King, keeper of the music room of the British Museum, who sent copies of those songs that are noted as from that collection; Miss Dorothy E. Mason, reference librarian of the Folger Shakespeare Library, Washington, for permitting me to see and copy songs from their collection of single-sheet songs; Mr. Robert O. Dougan, librarian of the Henry E. Huntington Library and Art Gallery, San Marino, California, for sending and granting permission to use the music for "Ally Croaker," "Come here, fellow Servant," and "Attend, all ye Fair," and for sending "There's not a Swain"; Mr. W. A. Taylor, librarian, the Shakespeare Memorial Library, Birmingham, England, for sending "Sabina with an Angel's Face"; Mr. Clifford Dodd, keeper of special collections, the Library of the University of Glasgow, Scotland, for "Ballynamony"; Mr. Oliver Davies, reference librarian of the Royal College of Music, London, for the "Solemn Dirge"; Dr. Edward M. Riley, director of research, and his staff of the Research Department, Colonial Williamsburg, for the use of the collection and for their cheerful and interested help in supplying and securing other materials. My thanks are extended to Dr. Edward P. Alexander, vice-president and director of interpretation, Colonial Williamsburg, for his interested advice, and to Mr. Carlton Sprague Smith for his helpful suggestions. To the staff of the Colonial Williamsburg Publications Department I extend the thanks they have earned in the editing, design, and production of this book.

I appreciate the assistance of the reference staff of the Earl Gregg Swem Library of the College of William and Mary in finding and supplying many of the play texts. To Mr. Charles Butler, librarian, and his staff at the Dabney S. Lancaster Library of Longwood College I extend my heart-felt thanks for their tireless assistance in acquiring materials through purchase and on interlibrary loan from other libraries in Virginia and throughout the country. I appreciate the assistance given me by the staffs of the University of Virginia Library, the Virginia Historical Society, the Virginia State Library, the Robert E. Lee Memorial Foundation, Stratford Hall, Stratford, and the Southern Historical Collection of the University of North Carolina.

Several persons gave of their time to answer inquiries, and I express my gratitude to them: Mr. R. J. Hayes, director of the National Library of Ireland, translated the song text of "Aileen Aroon"; Mrs. H. D. Hammitt, musical director of the John Judkyn Music Memorial, London, England, sent information concerning Woolls; Mr. W. H. N. Harding sent valuable information about songsters, *The Brent* in particular; and Mr. Clinton V. Black, archivist, Jamaica Archives, Spanish Town, Jamaica, sent information about Ann Hallam.

I also express my very deep appreciation to Mr. James S. Darling, organist and choirmaster of Bruton Parish Church, Williamsburg, for his careful review of, valuable suggestions concerning, and corrections to, the arrangements of the songs.

My son, John Edgar Molnar, displayed far more than filial duty in locating and securing materials, and in checking the bibliography and manuscript.

Finally, but by far the most important, my wholly inadequate thanks are given to my wife, Bonnie Hannaford Molnar, who worked countless hours in finding, reading, extracting, and compiling information, and in helping with the writing of the manuscript.

Longwood College
Farmville, Virginia

JOHN W. MOLNAR

Introduction

MUSIC held an important place on the stage of colonial Virginia beginning with the first theatre built in Williamsburg. The first in the English colonies in fact, it was erected in 1716 by William Levingston, a local merchant who kept a dancing school at the College of William and Mary. In Levingston's contract with Charles Stagg, an actor, violinist, and dancer, for the "better preparation of plays," it was agreed "that they bear equal share in all charges of cloathes, musick, and other necessaries for acting in plays. . . ." The agreement further stated that as Levingston "hath at his own proper cost and charge sent to England for actors and musicians for the better performance of the plays, it is agreed that . . . the same allowance shall be made for the musicians and actors as others equally qualified hired here in Virginia. . . ."

Two circumstances leave a clear implication that the short-lived company under the joint management of Walter Murray and Thomas Kean, who built Williamsburg's second theatre in 1751, used music in their performances there: Their New York advertisements the previous year mention it; shortly after the end of their Williamsburg season they used an amateur orchestra to accompany a performance of *The Beggar's Opera* in Maryland.

When Lewis Hallam's "Company of Comedians from London," the first successful colonial theatrical group, arrived in Williamsburg in 1752 to begin their American tour at the theatre taken over from the Murray–Kean Company, they announced that they were "perfected" in "all the best Plays, Opera's, Farces, and Pantomimes, that have been exhibited in any of the Theatres these ten years past." The company's announcement for their first performance stressed the songs in the play. Later bills continued the emphasis on music.

The American Company, successors to the Hallams, laid increasing importance on both instrumental and vocal music, as is apparent in their advertisements. Moreover, they added to their repertoire plays in which there was much music. David Douglass, the manager of the company, announced in 1766 that he had "collected some very eminent performers from both Theatres in London, particularly in the Singing Way, so that the English Comic Opera" (of which *Love in a Village* was the first) could be performed "to advantage." The company advertised the use of an orchestra for a performance of *Love in a Village* in Williamsburg in 1771. Even the short-lived Virginia Company used an orchestra for a performance of *The Beggar's Opera* there in 1768.

* * *

The Company of Comedians from London was a group organized on the English share-holding basis under the management of Lewis Hallam, one of an important eighteenth-century theatrical family whose members were numerous and active in the London and provincial theatres. His brother William was manager of the Goodman's Fields Theatre, one of the better nonpatent theatres in London, where the repertoire consisted of the same plays, "operas," and types of inter-act entertainment that the Hallams' colonial company presented.

In 1755 Lewis Hallam took his company to Jamaica, perhaps drawn there by the presence of Governor Sir Henry Moore, a patron of music and the theatre. In Jamaica, the Hallams combined with another troupe of players managed by David Douglass. After Lewis Hallam's death, Douglass married his widow, and in 1758 brought his players, who were to become the American Company, to New York to begin a series of tours that lasted until the Revolution. His company appeared in Annapolis and Williamsburg during the 1760–61 and 1762–63 seasons, including in their circuits stopover performances at other Maryland and Virginia towns. In 1770, 1771, and 1772, the company also gave series of performances in Williamsburg. One other group, known as the Virginia Company and the New American Company, played in Virginia and Maryland in 1768–69. Several of the players appeared with both the American and Virginia companies.

Although issues of the *Virginia Gazette* are incomplete for some of the periods during which the companies performed in Williamsburg, their seasonal repertoires are indicated in other colonial newspapers and surviving handbills. Diary, letter, and other indirect references help make definite the presence of the actors in Williamsburg.

* * *

The Williamsburg audience that greeted the opening performance of the Hallams' Company of Comedians would have been familiar with many of the play songs from presentations in the earlier theatre, from amateur productions, and from the Murray–Kean performances. Not only could the Virginians read theatrical news in their newspaper and in the periodicals to which they subscribed, but many an issue of such English periodicals as the *Gentleman's Magazine* and the *London Magazine*, contained the words and music of a song, often from one of the current plays. A number of Virginians had firsthand acquaintance with the finest of English theatre music through their visits to the playhouses when they were in London. Virginians' library inventories show they possessed the texts of the plays, and some of these, the ballad operas in particular, contained the music for the songs. The scores of the "operas" were available for purchase at the Williamsburg Printing Office, as advertised in the *Virginia Gazette*, or by means of orders placed by the colonists with their London agents. Many of the theatre songs were printed in such collections as D'Urfey's *Pills to Purge Melancholy*, Watts's *Musical Miscellany*, and Bickham's *Musical Entertainer*, copies of which were in Virginian homes. The colonials, in Virginia as elsewhere, copied the music of play songs into their manuscript music books in order to sing and play them for their own enjoyment, and records survive of their having had music books bound into volumes at the Printing Office.

* * *

The evening's entertainment seen by Williamsburg audiences followed the pattern of presentation that by mid-century had been established firmly and universally in the English-speaking theatre. The surviving handbills and advertisements of the colonial companies, when compared to those of the London and provincial theatres, show that the colonial companies presented the same plays and types of entertainment in all their aspects as did their Old World counterparts, and advertised them in almost identical language and form. The format of presentation was continued by the colonial troupes not only because it was the one they knew and in which they had always worked, but because their audiences, too, knew and expected it.

The program constituted one of varied and rich entertainment, designed to appeal to the taste of as broad a potential audience as possible. All elements of the format did not appear in every announcement. In all probability, however, some of its aspects were presented each evening, even when the bill stated only the bare essentials of the play and the afterpiece for that night. More of the pattern was evident in those bills that advertised the benefit performances, undoubtedly in order to attract as large a house as possible.

As shown in *The London Stage* and other sources, the pattern was full of music, and consisted in its entirety of:

(1) *The opening music*—how much the colonial companies provided is problematical, especially in the early period during the Murray–Kean and Hallam seasons;

(2) *A prologue*—usually spoken but sometimes sung, before the mainpiece;

(3) *The mainpiece*—a play of three to five acts, ranging from Shakespeare to recent contemporary works. The great majority of the plays in the repertoire demanded music in some form such as songs, dances, choruses, atmospheric background, and fanfares. The musical plays could not, of course, be performed at all without the music; this group included the quasi-operatic type such as *The Tempest*, the full length ballad operas such as *The Beggar's Opera*, and the "operas," actually operettas, such as *Love in a Village*;

(4) *An epilogue*—like the prologue, usually a part of the mainpiece and sometimes sung;

(5) *Dance*—in some form;

(6) *An afterpiece*—of one or two acts that might be farce, pantomime, or ballad or composed opera;

(7) *Popular vocal or instrumental music*—performed during the seven-minute intermissions between the acts and after the mainpiece; and

(8) *Specialty acts*—especially during the benefit season, in the form of individual or group dancing, instrumental or vocal music, rope dancing, and other types of entertainment that today would be called variety acts. Often the evening would conclude with a general dance by all the performers.

The efforts of the colonial players should not be compared to the performances at the great patent theatres in London—Drury Lane and Covent Garden, the pinnacle of theatrical achievement in the English-speaking world. Rather, they should be compared to those of the smaller London and town theatres, and to the touring provincial and summer suburban companies. In comparison to most of these, the Hallams and the American Company were in all probability at least as good.

The colonial players were not cast-offs from the English companies, but were competent actors. They were the type of substantial, all-round player, with the thorough training of the professional, that capably filled the secondary positions in the London theatres. They came to the colonies not only in search of employment but, especially in the case of the younger actors, in all probability in order to gain further experience. A study of the London, provincial, and Irish theatre casts shows the names of actors who came to America, and a number who returned, some to reach the actors' coveted goal, the stages of the patent theatres.

* * *

Only a brief mention is possible here of some of the styles represented by the songs in this selection. As can be expected of compositions from the period, there are frequent examples of tone painting; one is "Sabina with an Angel's Face." Recitative was not used extensively, but there are instances in the songs. "Sabina" again is an example; another is "The Early Horn." The latter, with "The Echoing Horn," is in the hunt style, highly popular with English audiences of the time. The sentimental style is represented by a number of songs, such as "When Damon languish'd," and the folk style is clearly seen in songs such as "Aileen Aroon."

In spite of the supposed antipathy of the English to Italian opera, arias were frequently taken from that genre and, with new words, were put into the plays. "Cupid, God of soft Persuasion" was set to the music of an aria of Giardini's, and Arne wrote his *Artaxerxes*, his own translation of a libretto by Metastasio, in the Italianate manner. An Italian agitato aria by Cocchi was appropriated for "My Passion in vain," and the style was cleverly satirized by Arne in his setting of "No Ice so hard."

Boyce, the traditionalist, wrote "If ever I'm catch'd" in a style already considered old-fashioned, while "Dear Heart," by Dibdin, was in the modern vein, with at least hints of Mozart's later comic opera idiom. Handel's "Let me wander not unseen" was used for "My Dolly was the fairest Thing" almost certainly because of the pensive mood of the music. The pre-Restoration solo song is represented by "Wher' did you borrow that last Sigh?" by Lawes.

The term "ballad opera" is something of a misnomer for a number of the plays of that type represented herein. These contained not only familiar tunes appropriated from the common currency, but also pieces especially composed for the play. Two examples are Carey's "Come hither my Country Squire" in his *The Honest Yorkshireman* and Seedo's "Ye Gods, Ye gave to me a Wife," written for Coffey's *The Devil to Pay*, a play that had important influence on the German *Singspiel*. A surprising number of the songs in the ballad operas were not "folk tunes" but music that has been traced to contemporary or older composers. Older music, as well as music recently written, was taken for the settings of new words. Apparently a good tune, no matter what its source and in the absence of effective copyright laws, was considered fair game for any musician setting the words in a play.

Such an adaptation of new words to a known melody, however, was not a haphazard affair. There are instances showing that the adapter chose the music with care to fit the emotional and dramatic situation and the rhythmic pattern of the new text. Often the tune, well-known to the audience, would indicate by its new use the meaning of the words and the situation, or sometimes reveal a humorous juxtaposition that was not lost on the audience.

A number of types of songs are included. "The Serenading Song" and many of the ballad opera songs carry forward the action of the play. Others, such as "Jessica's Song," describe or comment on the action. "Castalio's Complaint" and "She walks as she dreams" represent songs that create or intensify atmosphere and mood. Topical songs were introduced on occasion, particularly into the farces; "The Tragical History of the Life and Death of Billy Pringle's Pig" must have been such a song.

From mid-century on, the London theatre managers, imitated by their lesser counterparts including the colonial company's David Douglass, inserted more pageantry into their productions; this proved highly popular with their audiences. They introduced processions, usually with choral music, into those plays whose action and setting gave a plausible excuse for such spectacles. The "Solemn Dirge" in *Romeo and Juliet* is a famous example. The choruses that sang the music in these spectacular scenes were never large by modern standards, rarely numbering more than six to ten singers even at the patent theatres. The bills, both in England and in America, when naming the singers, invariably added an "etc." to the list of names, covering the possibility that other members of the company, or singers especially engaged for the performance, might sing in the chorus or reinforce the singers from off stage.

With the acquisition of more and better singers and instrumentalists, the colonial company added to its repertoire plays that demanded greater musical participation, as well as the new "operas" that were becoming increasingly popular in London. The increasing use of these full-length plays made it even more imperative that a capable actor should be able to sing.

The irrepressible British humor and penchant for satire is shown in *Midas*, an example of a burletta afterpiece. *The Musical Lady* not only ridiculed Italian opera, but is a valuable source of indirect information concerning the theatre music of the time. It and other plays give insight into the musical practices of the stage in the eighteenth century.

There are numerous examples of the interpolation of a song into a play. Sometimes the song was put into the play simply because it was popular, but usually the song was added because it fitted the action of the plot. "Aileen Aroon" was inserted into *Love a-la-Mode* in New York after Maria Storer had sung it successfully as an inter-act song, but "The Early Horn" had become an integral part of *The Devil to Pay* before the play was brought to America.

The playwrights used a number of devices to introduce songs and other music into their work.

One of the most transparent was that of calling on musicians or dancers to furnish entertainment for the characters when the action of the play called for a festive occasion. Occasionally the playwright gave the carte blanche direction, "Here, Musick," "A Song," or "Singing," thus permitting the use of available music or musicians. More often the author of the play provided a song text. Frequently, to ensure that the audience understood the words, the author would have the character recite the lyrics before singing the song, as in the case of "No Ice so hard."

Another device for the introduction of music was the use of a music master, often a comic figure. Sometimes the music master was a well-known musician playing himself, as, for instance, Carbonelli in *The Conscious Lovers*. *The Buck, or The Englishman in Paris* contains a scene in which Lucinda has a singing lesson under the tutelage of her music teacher, which gives a glimpse of the interpretation of music in the period.

Sometimes allowance was made for the song to be sung off stage, as in "The Serenading Song," or the stage directions instructed the actor to go off stage to sing the song, as in *The Lost Lady*. The device was used to permit the substitution of a good singer for an actor who could not meet the required standard of vocal performance. In other instances, as in *The Gamester* and *The Spanish Friar*, the song was sung by a servant, providing a situation, if necessary, in which a qualified singer could appear in a minor role that did not require great dramatic ability. Playwrights, particularly of farces, provided an excuse for those rare leading actors (of whom David Garrick was the most famous) who could not sing well by having the character apologize before singing his song, saying he had a cold or "I'm not in voice today," as in *High Life below Stairs*, *The Way to Keep Him*, and *Miss in Her Teens*.

The music in the plays was advertised in a number of ways. Both the English and the colonial advertisements frequently stated, following the name of the character in the play or the name of the actor playing the part, "Song(s) in Character," signifying that the music was a part of the role and was to be sung in the performance of the play. An example is found in the first advertisement in Williamsburg for *The Merchant of Venice* by the Hallam Company, which noted "Lorenzo, with Songs in Character, by Mr. Adcock."

"All Songs, Dances, and Decorations proper to the Play" assured the prospective audience that the music and dances that were a part of the play would be performed and that the required scenery would be used. "In Act I [etc.] will be sung" usually indicated that the music was a part of the play and was not inter-act entertainment. "The proper Song" was one that belonged in the play, and was not an interpolation; a "Song new set" meant a new musical version of the original words. "With a new Song" ordinarily meant new words and music, but a "Song introduced" into a role usually showed that it was already in existence and popular, as, for instance, "The Life of a Beau" in *The Miser*.

All the colonial companies had singers on their rolls. It was part of the professional actor's training to receive instruction in singing and often in playing an instrument. Most of the colonial actors could sing well enough to fulfill the requirements of at least a comic singing role that did not require the proficiency that a major role did, and a number of them were good enough to be featured as vocalists in the playbills and advertisements.

Nancy Hallam, Maria Storer, and Stephen Woolls especially became favorites of the colonial audiences, not only in the theatre but on concert programs. The colonial singers, like their London counterparts, often appeared in concerts in the cities where the company was appearing. Singing actors who were primarily actors but who sang acceptably included Lewis Hallam, Jr., Thomas Wall, Mrs. Harman, and others.

The colonial companies had instrumentalists to furnish the accompaniment for the singing in the plays and between the acts. On occasion, probably only one or two were used, but the colonial troupes were not different in this limitation in their resources from the smaller companies in England of the day. It is difficult to find the names or numbers of the English orchestral players even in connection with the large patent theatres, since the names of the musicians appear in the London bills only when they were featured as soloists between the acts, and because very few lists of instrumental performers apparently have survived.

In the colonies, the names of several instrumentalists with the company or in theatre-connected concerts have been found. Undoubtedly others were available, since notices state that the music would be "conducted by [i.e., in charge of] Mr. Pelham and others," or that Mr. Hallam would conduct the orchestra. Usually the only source is found in the names of musicians who were on the periphery of the company; it can hardly be called coincidence that the names of instrumentalists appear in advertisements to teach and give concerts at the time and in the locality in which the company was active.

By 1760 the American Company had the necessary musical resources to present larger works that demanded considerable vocal and instrumental music, such as *Theodosius* and *The Tempest*. Extra musicians were used whenever they were available to augment the company's forces. The resident church musicians, music teachers, and members of the military and naval bands that might be stationed nearby provided a constant source of personnel. Gentlemen amateurs offered or were requested to play in the orchestra, especially on "opera nights."

The ballad operas and afterpieces could have been presented, and in all probability were on many an occasion, with little more than a harpsichord or spinet for accompaniment. The scores for these plays were modest in their instrumental demands, usually calling for little more than first and second violins, and a flute or oboe (usually doubled by one player), with, of course, a cello or string bass for the bass line. The bass instruments were so assumed to be elements of the ensemble that they were not mentioned in the advertisements of the scores. Nor was a separate part usually written for them, the player reading the bass line from the harpsichord score.

In the latter half of the period, when presenting the more elaborate musical plays, the orchestra was undoubtedly larger. It would consist of the basic instruments mentioned above plus several extra violins on the two parts, perhaps a viola, and another cello or bass with the very probable addition of a bassoon on the bass line. The woodwinds would be augmented by another flute and oboe, and in the case of *Thomas and Sally*, two clarinets. Two horns would complete the orchestra. The harpsichord, the basic instrument of all ensembles of the period, was always included.

Very probably the complete roster of instruments was not always available, so the conductor had to rewrite and transfer parts to those instruments that were present, or play the missing parts on the harpsichord, at which he presided at the performance. The term "conductor" did not signify the baton-waving interpreter of today; instead, it meant the leader in charge of the musical performance as a whole. The position he occupied can be compared roughly to a combination of offices in one of today's musical organizations.

Even if the company was large enough for him to delegate some of the tasks, he was responsible for the personnel and business management of the instrumentalists, securing needed players in addition to those who were with the company. He would transpose songs and orchestra parts to fit the singers' voices, writing out or altering the orchestra music to conform to the available instrumentation, and he would coach the singers. In addition, he was the harpsichordist-leader at the performance, playing the chords, cuing and supporting the singers (by playing their parts if they failed or faltered), and keeping things together and moving by indications of a free hand, his head, or when necessary, his feet.

The company must have carried their own music library with them. They could have procured the music either in manuscript from one of the English theatres, by purchase or loan of the printed scores, or by arranging the orchestral parts from the music of the songs that were frequently printed in single-sheet form, in the play scripts, or in the periodicals.

* * *

It seemed fitting to use for the first song in this collection the light-hearted "The Trifle," sung in *The Beaux' Stratagem*, one of the first plays to be seen by colonial Williamsburg audiences. It, like many of the other fifty songs, is like much theatre music, ephemeral but effective in its setting. Others are appealing, and some are beautiful; a number of them could well bear revival today.

The next two songs are from *The Merchant of Venice*, the first play performed in Williamsburg by the Hallam Company in September 1752, when they started their American tour. Thereafter, no particular order is observed in the sequence of songs, except that whenever a mainpiece and afterpiece are known to have been performed on the same bill in Williamsburg, the songs from the two plays are placed together. Thus, for example, the two *Merchant of Venice* songs are followed by that from *High Life below Stairs*.

The most appropriate song to end the selection is without doubt the "Epilogue Song" to *The Irish Widow*, not only because of the theatrical connotation but because it was sung in one of the last plays to be introduced into colonial America.

[1]

The Trifle

sung in

THE BEAUX' STRATAGEM

A Comedy by George Farquhar

George Farquhar (1678–1707) *Daniel Purcell (ca. 1660–1717)*

In a trifling manner

mp
near, And I shall be nob - ly at - tend - ed. Were it
p
not for Tri - fles a few, That late - ly have come in - to
mf
play, Men wou'd want some - thing to do, And
mp
Wo - men want some-thing to say!
f

2

What makes a Man trifle in dressing?
Because the Ladies, they know,
Admire, by often possessing,
That eminent Trifle, a Beau.
When the Lover his Moments has trifled,
The Trifle or Trifles to gain,
No sooner the Virgin is rifled,
But the Trifle shall part 'em again.

3

What mortal Man wou'd be able
At White's half an hour to sit?
Or who cou'd bear a Tea-Table
Without talking of Trifles for Wit?
The Court is from Trifles secure—
Gold Keys are no Trifles, we see,
White Rods are no Trifles, I'm sure—
Whatever their Bearers may be.

4

But if you will go to the Place
Where Trifles abundantly breed,
The Levee will show you His Grace
Makes Promises Trifles indeed.
A Coach with six Footmen behind
I count neither Trifle nor Sin,
But, Ye Gods! how oft do we find
A scandalous Trifle within.

5

The Stage is a Trifle, they say,
The Reasons, pray, carry along;
Because at every new Play
The House they with Trifles so throng.
But with People's Malice to trifle,
And to set us all on a Foot:
The Author of this is a Trifle,
And his Song is a Trifle to boot!

"THE TRIFLE" was the wry and witty summation of himself and his world that George Farquhar provided as a song text for *The Beaux' Stratagem*, the eighth and last of his increasingly successful plays. In the throes of his final illness, depressed and penniless because an influential patron had failed to provide him with a promised army commission, Farquhar received from his friend Robert Wilks, the noted actor, twenty guineas and encouragement to finish his comedy. When the play was produced in the spring of 1707, shortly before the author's death at the age of twenty-nine, Wilks in his role of Archer sang "The Trifle."[1]

The song is performed by Archer in his disguise as his friend Aimwell's servant. These scheming young gentlemen from London, believing that rags are a scandal and poverty a crime, pretend to be a wealthy master and his servant as they travel in search of rich heiresses to mend their broken fortunes. While thus playing the menial, Archer shares a tankard of ale and a few songs with Scrub, a serving man, who is so impressed with the vocal ability of his new acquaintance that he commends it to his mistress, the wealthy and unhappily married Mrs. Sullen, and to her sister-in-law, Dorinda. When the ladies request Archer to sing, he pertly inquires if they are for "passion or humour." Scrub suggests his friend's "purest ballad about a trifle," and Archer, professing himself reluctant to offer Mrs. Sullen so trifling a song, finally obliges.

"The Trifle" was printed in 1718 in "The Life and Character of Mr. George Farquhar," where it was described as "justly esteemed one of the most humourous Pieces of its Kind extant in the English Language."[2]

Daniel Purcell's setting of "The Trifle" appeared in single-sheet form about 1707 and proved popular enough to be selected by John Watts, the publisher, for volume four of his song collection, *The Musical Miscellany*.[3]

The Beaux' Stratagem, which rivaled Farquhar's *The Recruiting Officer* in popularity,[4] was one of the first identified plays to be given in Williamsburg, being performed there in 1736 "by the Gentlemen and Ladies of this Country";[5] it could have been one of the unidentified plays given at Williamsburg's first theatre, which was built about 1716. Other colonial performances were recorded before 1752 when the Hallam Company arrived with the play in their repertoire. It remained a favorite with audiences until the end of the colonial period.

Archer in the Hallam's first season was played by John Singleton, a name associated with them in the casts of their Goodman's Fields Theatre in London in 1744, and mentioned there as late as 1749.[6] An actor, violinist, and poet, he advertised to teach the violin "to Gentlemen and others" shortly after the company's arrival in Williamsburg.[7] He was no longer with the company on its return from Jamaica in 1758 under the new management of David Douglass. Lewis Hallam, Jr., who in 1754 had made his colonial debut at the age of 14 as an inter-act singer in his father's company, took over the part of Archer in the colonial performances of the play after 1758.[8]

[2]

The Serenade

sung in

THE MERCHANT OF VENICE

Adapted from the Play by William Shakespeare

Sir Richard Steele (1672–1729) — *Thomas A. Arne (1710–1778)*

long my Bride de - nies, A -
pace the waft - - ing Sum - mer
flies; Nor yet the Wint - - 'ry
blasts I fear nor Storms or
tr
tr
6
6
5
6
5
6
6
6
5
6
6
7
6
5
7
6
6

2

What may for Strength with Steel compare,
Oh, Love has Fetters stronger far!
By bolts of Steel are Limbs confin'd,
But cruel Love enchains the Mind.

3

No longer then perplex thy Breast,
When thoughts torment the first are best,
'Tis mad to go, 'tis Death to stay,
Away to Jesse, haste away.

THE sensation of the London theatre world just before mid-century was the new Drury Lane version of *The Merchant of Venice*. This was the play Lewis Hallam and his Company of Comedians chose for their first American performance on the night of September 15, 1752, at Williamsburg. The part of Lorenzo, played by William Adcock, was billed "with Songs in Character," a notation long established in London playbills and soon to become familiar in America, where the play held a place in the repertoire until 1774. A second performance was recorded in Williamsburg in 1768 when the Virginia Company presented it, with *High Life below Stairs* as the afterpiece.[1]

The play was not as written by Shakespeare but was closer to his original than the version it replaced—Lansdowne's truncated and never very popular *The Jew of Venice*. At the first performance of the new version, Charles Macklin, creating the role in which he was to triumph for the next fifty years, portrayed Shylock as so malevolent that George II suggested to Robert Walpole using the actor to frighten the House of Commons.[2]

Thomas Arne, the Drury Lane composer then at the auspicious beginning of his career, provided the music for the new production, and published his two interpolated songs for Lorenzo, "The Serenade" and "To Keep my gentle Jessie," in one of his song collections. Both became popular and were reprinted in other collections and in less expensive single-sheet form until the end of the century.[3] Lorenzo sings "The Serenade" to Jessica in Act II, scene 6, which takes place before the house of her father, Shylock.

Although Thomas Lowe, the London actor and singer, was the performer most frequently identified with the role of Lorenzo and the songs, in later years George Mattocks, a singing actor at Covent Garden and brother-in-law of Lewis Hallam, Jr., of the American Company, was featured in the role "with Songs."[4]

William Adcock, who played Lorenzo in the premier American performance, was the Hallam Company's principal singer; he had just married Mary Palmer, an actress with the troupe. He and his wife later appeared at the Haymarket and at Drury Lane in London, and at the Crow Street Theatre in Dublin and elsewhere in Ireland, from 1757 to 1765. When Arne's pupil, Stephen Woolls, became the American Company's featured singer, he too played Lorenzo "with Songs."[5]

[3]

Jessica's Song

sung in

THE MERCHANT OF VENICE

Adapted from the Play by William Shakespeare

Unidentified — *Joseph Baildon (ca. 1727–1774)*

To my long - ing Arms re - pair,
With im - pa - tience
I shall die,
Come and ease thy Jes - sie's care.
Let me then in
wan - ton Play
Sigh and gaze my Soul a - way,

Sigh and gaze my Soul a - way,
mf
Sigh, and gaze my Soul a - way.
p
pp
Let me then in wan - ton
tr
Play, Sigh and gaze,
ad lib.
colla voce

JESSICA'S appealing song was inserted at the end of scene 5 in Act II. Jessica, preparing to elope with Lorenzo, has disobeyed her father's order to "bind fast" the door at his departure. Her closing lines, "Farewell—and if my fortune be not crost, I have a father, you a daughter, lost," precede her song.

The song was set by Joseph Baildon, a lay vicar of Westminster Abbey, who was elected organist of St. Luke's Church, Old Street, about the time his song collection *The Laurel* was published.[1]

Songs for Jessica, in addition to those for Lorenzo, were mentioned in the bills by 1746, when Miss Edwards was announced in the role "in which will be performed several new songs proper to the Character."[2] Baildon's song was popular enough to be republished as late as 1770.

At the first performance of the play in Williamsburg Mrs. Rigby played Jessica. Her husband also was a member of the Hallam Company. A later Jessica was Miss Wainwright, who joined the American Company in 1765 and was featured in many singing roles. A pupil of Arne, she had made her stage debut in his *The Guardian Outwitted* at Covent Garden in December 1764. She appeared for the first time in the colonies with Nancy Hallam, also a newcomer, at a benefit concert for Peter Valton, organist at St. Philip's Church, Charleston, on November 13, 1765.[3]

Miss Hallam and Maria Storer also played Jessica with the American Company. In the Virginia Company's performance of the play in Williamsburg in 1768, the role probably was taken by Mrs. Parker.[4]

[4]

Come Here, Fellow Servant

sung in

HIGH LIFE BELOW STAIRS

A Comedy by James Townley

James Townley (1714–1778) *Jonathan Battishill (1738–1801)*

bet - ter than we, Are on - ly de - pen - dants, no bet - ter than we. Both
high and low in this do a - gree, 'Tis here, fel - low Ser - vant, and
there, fel - low Ser - vant, and all in a li - - ve - ry.
CHORUS
'Tis
f
here, fel - low Ser - vant, and there, fel - low Ser - vant, And all in a li - - ve -

2

See yonder fine spark, in embroidery dress'd
Who bows to the great, and, if they smile, is blest;
Who is he? i'faith, but a Servant at best,
Both high, etc.

3

Nature made all alike, no distinction she craves,
So we laugh at the great world, its fools, and its knaves;
For we are all Servants, but they are all slaves,
Both high, etc.

4

The fat shining glutton looks up to his shelf,
The wrinkled lean miser bows down to his pelf,
And the curl-pated beau is a slave to himself,
Both high, etc.

5

The gay sparkling belle who the whole town alarms,
And with eyes, lips, and neck sets the smarts all in arms,
Is a vassal herself, a meer drudge to her charms,
Both high, etc.

6

Then we'll drink like our betters and laugh, sing, and love,
And when sick of one place, to another we'll move,
For with little and great, the best joy is to rove,
Both high, etc.

IN the absence of their master, and with his friends' servants as guests, the housemaid Kitty and her fellow servants give a supper and dance. But the master, suspecting his staff of dishonesty, has only pretended to visit his country estate. Instead he watches the frolic from concealment as the servants assume the names and titles as well as the manners of their respective masters and mistresses.

Kitty asks the fiddler to play "Marshall Thingumbob's Minuet" and "Sir Harry" dances it with her.[1] After the dance "the Duke" calls for the song composed by "Sir Harry," who in turn requests Kitty to "honour my Muse" by singing it. She protests that she is really hoarse, "but—Hem—I must clear my pipes. This is Sir Harry's Song, being a new Song entitled and call'd 'The Fellow Servant, or All in a Livery'." All the servants join in the chorus. The master's sudden appearance brings confusion and dismissal.

The Reverend James Townley, a clergyman and schoolmaster who was a friend of David Garrick and a frustrated dramatist, wrote the farce in 1759.[2]

The music to Kitty's song was Jonathan Battishill's earliest contribution to the stage. A former chorister at St. Paul's, he was shortly—in 1761, at twenty-three—to be elected to the Royal Society of Music. Soon afterwards he became harpsichordist at Covent Garden Theatre, where he met and married a singing actress, Miss Davis or Davies, the original Margery in *Love in a Village*. According to a younger contemporary he was remembered as "poor Batt," gifted but eccentric.[3]

The part of Kitty apparently was designed for Kitty Clive, the popular actress who played it. Mrs. Clive's ability to project a song was such that authors frequently tailored parts and lyrics to suit her. In the colonies the first actress identified with the role was Margaret Cheer, who appeared in it with the American Company in the 1767 season in Philadelphia. A "Gentleman Contributor" of a letter to the *Pennsylvania Gazette* praised her sweet accent and clarity of expression and avowed that "she well fits the highest character she ever assumes." Her reported marriage in 1768 to Lord Rosehill, heir to the Earl of Northesk, who had been in Philadelphia the preceding winter, remains an unsolved biographical puzzle; she continued to appear on the stage under her maiden name as late as 1773.[4]

Miss Cheer alternated in the role of Kitty with Ann

Storer Henry, who had appeared in 1756 and 1759 on the Irish stage with her parents, Charles and Elizabeth Clark Storer. Ann's youngest sister, Maria, was assigned the song in later performances in Philadelphia and New York, though the role she played was that of another servant.[5]

Ann, Maria, and a third sister, Fannie, and their brother-in-law, John Henry, were the only members of the family to survive a fire at sea en route from Jamaica to New York in 1767. Mrs. Storer, a well-known singer in Ireland, had taken her family to Jamaica in 1763; she perished with her daughter, Mrs. Henry, and the two Henry children. Henry and his two sisters-in-law joined the American Company. He married Ann about 1769, and after the Revolution took Maria as his third Storer wife.[6]

The Virginia Company performed *High Life below Stairs* in Williamsburg in May of 1768 as an afterpiece to *The Merchant of Venice*, but the announcement in the *Virginia Gazette* gave no cast.[7]

[5]

My Heart Was so Free

sung in

THE BEGGAR'S OPERA

A Ballad Opera by John Gay

John Gay (1685–1732) *Richard Leveridge (1670–1758)*

Come, Fair One, Be Kind

sung in

THE RECRUITING OFFICER

A Comedy by George Farquhar

George Farquhar (1678–1707) *Richard Leveridge*

Heart was so free, It rov'd like a Bee, Till Pol - ly my Pas - sion re -
fair One, be kind, You ne - ver shall find, A Fel low so fit for a
qui - ted. I sipt each Flow'r, I chang'd ev' - ry Hour, I
Lo - ver. The World shall view My Pas - sion for you, The
sipt each Flow'r, I chang'd ev' - ry Hour, But here ev' - ry
World shall view my Pas - sion for you, But ne - ver your
Flow'r is u - ni - ted. I sipt each Flow'r, I chang'd ev' - ry
Pas - sion dis - co - ver. The World shall view my Pas - sion for

Hour, I sipt each Flow'r, I chang'd ev' - ry Hour, But
you, The World shall view my Pas - sion for you, But
Beggar's Opera ending. Fine
Recruiting Officer.
here ev' - ry Flow'r is u - ni - ted.
ne - ver your Pas - sion dis - - - - - - - co - ver.
p
I still will com - plain of Frowns and Dis - dain, Tho' I
re - vel through all your Charms, I still will com - plain of

Frowns and Dis - dain, 'Tho' I re - vel through all your Charms. The
World shall de - clare I die with Des - pair, Yes, I
die with Des - pair, Yes, I die with Des - pair,
When on - ly I die in your Arms, When

(rit.)
(a tempo)
on - ly I die in your Arms I still will a - dore, And
(rit.)
(a tempo)
love more and more, But by Jove, if you chance to be cru - el, I'll
get me a Miss that free - ly will kiss, I'll get me a Miss that
free - ly will kiss, Tho' af - ter, I drink Wat - er Gru - el.

THESE two song texts from plays nearly a quarter of a century apart, set to the same tune, demonstrate the way that music arrangers of ballad operas appropriated popular tunes for their own purposes. In this instance, the air that Richard Leveridge composed for "Come, fair One, be kind," Captain Plume's Act III song in George Farquhar's *The Recruiting Officer* of 1706, was "borrowed" in 1728 for "My Heart was so free" in *The Beggar's Opera*, the first of the popular new genre, the ballad opera.

The tune was one of sixty-nine that came under Peter Pelham's musical supervision when the newly organized Virginia Company gave the first performance of *The Beggar's Opera* recorded in Williamsburg on June 3, 1768. According to the playbill, the role of Captain Macheath, the highwayman who sings this song, was played by William Verling, it "being his first appearance in that Character." Verling, a former member of the American Company, was the organizer and manager of the new troupe.[1]

The bill also promised that "the Musick of the Opera will be conducted by Mr. Pelham and others." As conductor in the eighteenth-century meaning of the term, Pelham, organist of Bruton Parish Church in Williamsburg and teacher of harpsichord, would have co-ordinated the entire musical part of the production. In this, according to custom, he should have had the help of the "first violin" (in modern terms, the concertmaster), whose duty was to keep an eye and ear on the playing of the other members of the band, or, as it was beginning to be known, the orchestra.[2]

The participation of a church organist in a theatre performance was not unusual. It was customary for eighteenth-century musicians, especially organists, to divide their activities between the church and stage. However, it is doubtful if Pelham followed the example of his contemporary, William Tuckey, organist of Trinity Church in New York, who played Peachum in a performance of *The Beggar's Opera* given by the American Company at which the "original overture" was played.[3]

The overture was composed by that "excellent musician" Dr. John Christopher Pepusch, who arranged and set the basses (i.e., harmonized the melodies) for Gay's songs. Many of the tunes were selected because of the connotations they conveyed to the audience from their original settings.[4]

John Gay's ballad opera, which enjoyed instantaneous success in 1728, changed the course of the eighteenth-century stage. His own success in writing song lyrics has been attributed to his knowledge of music. A poet, dramatist, and amateur flautist, Gay had been educated at the Barnstaple grammar school in Devon, where the headmaster, the Reverend Robert Luck, instilled in his pupils his own interest in music and drama.[5]

Although no surviving record shows a performance of the opera in the colonies before 1750, its combination of tunefulness, novelty, gibes at Italian opera, political satire, and parody of the social order, which appealed to all varieties of taste, generated interest in Virginia within a few years after it began its meteoric career. In 1732 William Byrd II of Westover plantation, who often attended the theatre when in England, called at Tuckahoe, the Randolph home near the present Richmond, Virginia. There he read to the family from their copy of *The Beggar's Opera*, and regaled them with gossip about its background.[6]

Not all Virginians were pleased with the play. A volume of *Poems on Several Occasions*, "the casual productions of youth," by "A Gentleman of Virginia," was printed in 1736 in Williamsburg by William Parks. The author has been identified as the Reverend William Dawson, president of the College of William and Mary from 1743 to 1752. In verses "On the Corruptions of the Stage" he credits Macheath with routing Harlequin and the Italian opera, but criticizes him for starting the "raging frenzy" by which "From foreign trifling and unmanly Tone/We turn to downright Nonsense of our own."[7]

The first colonial notice that paid attention to the music in the opera was an announcement of a Masonic benefit performance at Upper Marlborough, a Maryland county seat, in 1752 by the Murray-Kean Company. The troupe under the management of Walter Murray and Thomas Kean had recently finished playing in Williamsburg, where they also may have given it.[8] The Maryland performance was enhanced by "A Set of Private Gentlemen providing the Instrumental Musick to each Air."[9]

The last recorded colonial performance of *The Beggar's Opera* in Williamsburg was given by the American Company when they opened the theatre with it for the season on June 14, 1770. The following winter the *Virginia Gazette* advertised the printed opera "set to Musick."[10]

[6]

Sweet Is the Budding Spring of Love

sung in

FLORA, or HOB IN THE WELL

A Ballad Opera adapted by John Hippisley

John Hippisley (d. 1748)

Unidentified

when pos - sess'd of Beau - ty's Charms, Fru -
i - tion, like the Sum - mer, warms. But Plea - sures, oft re -
peat - ed, cloy, To Au - tumn wanes the fleet - ing Joy, De -
clin - ing 'til De - sires are lost, Suc - ceed - ed by E -

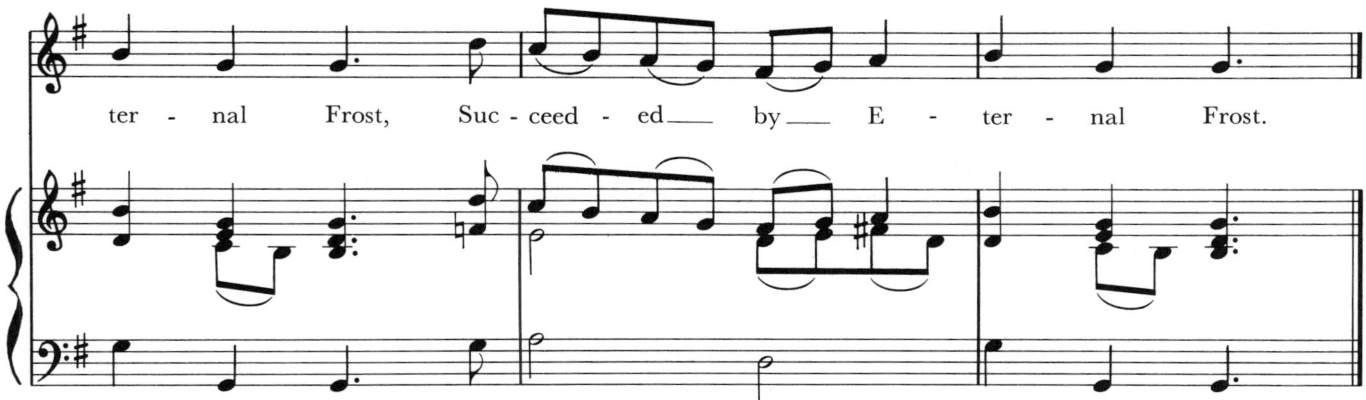

FLORA, or Hob in the Well was one of the ballad farces the Hallam Company "cast and studied for the common stock" before they left London for Virginia in 1752. The first ballad opera known to have been given on the American stage, it had been performed in Charleston seventeen years earlier and remained popular throughout the colonial period.[1]

The farce, which centers on the rowdy antics of the clownish Hob, had been adapted in 1729 by John Hippisley from the one-act afterpiece altered in 1711 from Thomas Doggett's play of 1696, *The Country Wake*. Hippisley, the original Peachum in *The Beggar's Opera*, was among the first of Gay's many imitators in realizing the possibilities in the ballad opera's appeal. He supplied the farce with lyrics for twenty-five songs. The tunes chosen for them did not, for the most part, duplicate the sixty-nine airs pre-empted by *The Beggar's Opera*.[2]

Flora sings "Sweet is the budding Spring of Love" in the final scene, when all the characters are assembled at a fair. A noisy quarrel between Hob and Flora's uncle and guardian, Sir Thomas Testy, has given her the chance to slip away and marry her lover, Friendly. When the newlyweds return to the scene, Flora answers her bridegroom's protestations of eternal love with this skeptical song.[3]

Four singing actresses are known to have played Flora in the colonies. The first was Mrs. Becceley, who joined the Hallam Company from the defunct Murray-Kean group, with whom she played in Virginia. The others were Nancy Hallam, the young Maria Storer, and Sarah, the first wife of Lewis Hallam, Jr. Mrs. Hallam appeared with the company in New York during the winter of 1761–62, between the group's Maryland-Virginia tours of 1760–61 and 1762–63. Flora was one of the several singing roles in which she was cast. She may have been with the company during the 1760–61 season, when they gave *Flora, or Hob in the Well* in Annapolis, no doubt repeating it in Williamsburg during the ensuing fall and winter.[4]

After the marriage foundered, Sarah Hallam remained in Williamsburg. She opened a popular dancing school in 1775 at the house of Blovet Pasteur, and lived in the colonial capital a respected citizen, until her death in 1793.[5]

For the Hallams the opera had early associations. The author, "the agreeable and facetious Mr. Hippisley," had shared a theatrical booth with William Bullock, the noted actor, and one of the elder Hallams—probably Adam—at Bartholomew Fair in 1734, when Lewis Hallam, Sr., appeared with their company as Master Hallam. He later played Hob at the Hallam's theatre in Goodman's Fields in 1749, in a company that included Singleton and Malone—names that were to appear on the company's bills when it arrived in Virginia three years later. Lewis Hallam, and his son Lewis, each performed "Mr. Hippisley's humourous Scene of a Drunken Man" as an inter-act piece on the colonial stage.[6]

[7]

A Soldier and a Sailor

sung in

LOVE FOR LOVE

A Comedy by William Congreve

William Congreve (1670–1729) — *John Eccles (1668–1735)*

A Fox May Steal Your Hens, Sir

sung in

THE BEGGAR'S OPERA

A Ballad Opera by John Gay

John Gay (1685–1732) — *John Eccles*

(**Lively**)

f *mf*

[*Love for Love*] A Sol - dier and__ a

[*Beggar's Opera*] A fox__ may steal__ your

once a doubt - - ful Strife, Sir, To make a Maid a
daught - er rob your Chest, Sir, Your Wife may steal your
Wife, Sir, Whose Name was Bux - - - om Joan,
Rest, Sir, A Thief your Goods and Plate,
f
Whose Name was Bux - om Joan For
A Thief your Goods and Plate. But
mf
now the Time is end - - - ed when she no more in-
this is all but pick - - ing With Rest, Pence, Chest, and

tend - - - ed to lick her Chops at Men, Sir, And
Chick - - - en, If ev - - - er was de - creed, Sir, If
gnaw the Sheets in vain, Sir,
Law - - yer's Hand is fee'd, Sir,
And lie o' Nights a - lone,
He steals your whole Es - tate,
And lie o' Nights a - lone.
He steals your whole Es - tate.

A SOLDIER AND A SAILOR

2

The Soldier swore like Thunder,
He lov'd her more than Plunder,
And show'd her many a Scar, Sir,
That he had brought from far, Sir,
   With fighting for her sake.
The Tailor thought to please her
With offering her his Measure.
The Tinker, too, with Mettle
Said he wou'd mend her Kettle
   And stop up ev'ry Leak.

3

But while these three were prating,
The Sailor slyly waiting,
Thought if it came about, Sir,
That they shou'd all fall out, Sir,
   He then might play his Part.
And just e'en as he meant, Sir,
To Loggerheads they went, Sir,
And then he let fly at her
A shot 'twixt Wind and Water,
   That won this fair Maid's Heart.

MRS. FRAIL, a "Woman of the Town" in Congreve's play, has set her matrimonial course for Ben, the "half home-bred, half sea-bred" son of Sir Sampson Legend, thinking him to be his father's heir. Vowing that he is "not false-hearted like a landsman," Ben sings her this "Song for a Sailor that the Boatswain made upon one of the Wives of the Ship's Crew, Buxom Joan of Deptford." At the end of it he whistles to summon his shipmates "and Fiddles along with them." The appearance of the violinists on stage illustrates the custom of using members of the theatre's band (i.e., the orchestra) as participants in such scenes as this.[1]

Ben's song proved enduringly popular. Its tune was chosen for one of the airs in Gay's *The Beggar's Opera*. To it Peachum sings "A Fox may steal your Hens, Sir" as part of his complaint against lawyers who "don't care that any Body should get a Clandestine Livelihood but themselves." The tune was also used for other ballad operas and was reprinted with the original words as late as 1739.[2] The song was in such demand that an audience at a Drury Lane performance of *Love for Love* in 1754 hissed Samuel Foote when he wouldn't sing it, although he explained that he had no talent for singing. Changing tastes in the latter part of the eighteenth century demanded some cutting of the play, but Ben's song—of the three originally included—survived. However, the gestures that traditionally accompanied it presumably were "expunged."[3]

Congreve wrote Ben's part and song for the comical talents of the lively Thomas Doggett, who prepared for his role by lodging near the Thames at Wapping and haunting the docks there to learn sailor speech and ways. Congreve's favorite composer, John Eccles, an ardent fisherman who shared Doggett's interest in the Thames, set the music for Ben's nautical song. A prolific theatre composer, Eccles also set other playhouse songs for Doggett.[4]

Williamsburg playgoers may have seen *Love for Love* before the Hallam Company arrived in 1752. The Murray-Kean troupe had the play in their repertoire in 1751, and it may have been among the plays performed at the first theatre. Perhaps it was one of the unidentified three that William Byrd II attended there in 1721.[5]

The play would have been no novelty to the wealthy, cultured, and worldly squire of Westover plantation. Three decades earlier he had entered London's Middle Temple to study law while William Congreve, then in his early twenties, was still there. When *Love for Love* opened the new playhouse at Lincoln's Inn Fields on April 30, 1695, Byrd may have been in the audience. Certainly he did attend a London performance in 1718, but the company wasn't lively enough to keep him awake.[6]

The first identified Ben in the colonies was the senior Lewis Hallam, who was familiar with the role before his company arrived in Virginia in 1752. He had played it at the Hallam's Goodman's Fields Theatre near London as early as six years before. After his death his son inherited the role. In March 1762, during the New York season, young Hallam was billed as "Ben the Sailor, with a Song in Character," a performance undoubtedly also offered to the audiences of Williamsburg.[7]

Some of Virginia's theatregoers possessed the play in their libraries. Colonel Byrd's library at Westover included the three-volume octavo edition of Congreve's works (first published in 1710). The estate settlement of Colonel John Waller of Spotsylvania, father of Judge Benjamin Waller of Williamsburg, shows that he had the song and perhaps the play. His estate contained music, instruments, poems, and plays—including a volume of Congreve's works—as well as *Pills to Purge Melancholy*, in which Ben's song appears in all editions. The library of Thomas Jefferson, whose varied interests extended to music and the theatre, included the Glasgow edition of Congreve's *Dramatic Works* of 1761.[8]

[8]

O All Ye Powers Above

sung in

THE VIRGIN UNMASK'D, or THE OLD MAN TAUGHT WISDOM

A Ballad Opera by Henry Fielding

Henry Fielding (*1707–1754*)

John Eccles (*1668–1735*)

A WEALTHY country squire, who would like to keep his money in the family, tries to persuade his daughter Lucy, whom he has sheltered from the world, to choose one of their poor relations for a husband. Lucy, more knowing than her father thinks, looks them all over and decides that she wants to marry the footman, Thomas, with whom, as her song shows, she has fallen in love.

Henry Fielding's farce was a popular afterpiece for many seasons after its first performance in 1735.[1] Its nineteen tunes were selected from those in *The Beggar's Opera* and other ballad pieces, including several of Fielding's own. Lucy's song was set to an air that had retained its popularity since John Eccles composed it forty years earlier for "Ye Nymphs and Sylvan Gods," one of the songs in part II of Thomas D'Urfey's play *Don Quixote*. D'Urfey's words were a reworking of a song text by Martin Parker set to an old tune, "The Merry Milk-Maids." D'Urfey printed the song in his *Pills to Purge Melancholy* "as sung in my play of *Don Quixote*."[2] George Farquhar later borrowed a snatch of the song for his play, *The Recruiting Officer*.[3]

Eccles's air was heard in other ballad operas performed in the colonies besides *The Virgin Unmask'd*, including

Fielding's *The Mock Doctor*, where it was used for Air 8, "The Soldier who bravely goes." Two years earlier, in 1730, it had been taken as the tune to "My Humours frank and free," for Charles Coffey's ballad opera, *The Beau in the Suds, or The Female Parson.*[4]

The Virgin Unmask'd, an early and often repeated afterpiece on the colonial stage, was first performed before the arrival of the Hallam Company in 1752, who also had it in their repertoire. It was undoubtedly frequently performed in Williamsburg.[5]

The role of Lucy, first played in England by Kitty Clive, was performed by several of the colonial actresses. Miss Hallam, variously identified as either the sister or the eldest daughter of Lewis Hallam, played the part in New York in 1753. Later Lucys were the first Mrs. Owen Morris and Catherine Maria Harman, a third-generation member of an English theatrical family. At fourteen she had played with her mother, the flamboyant Charlotte Cibber Charke, with the Hallam Company at the London fairs.[6]

[9]

Over the Hills and Far Away

sung in

THE RECRUITING OFFICER

A Comedy by George Farquhar

Unidentified *Unidentified*

2

We all shall lead more happy lives
By getting rid of brats and wives
That scold and brawl both night and day—
Over the hills and far away.
Refrain:
Over the hills, and o'er the main, &c.

3

Courage, boys, 'tis one to ten,
But we return all gentlemen,
All gentlemen as well as they,
Over the hills and far away.
Refrain:
Over the hills, &c.

SNATCHES from a song beginning "Hark! now the Drums beat up again/For all true Soldiers Gentlemen" were sung repeatedly during the recruiting scene that ends the second act of Farquhar's comedy. They consisted, as given here, of the tenth, twelfth, and fourteenth verses and refrain, and were printed in the play published four days after the first performance in 1706. The complete song text was published in *Pills to Purge Melancholy* either earlier or later that same year, where it was specified to be sung to the tune of "Jockey's Lamentation."[1]

The composer of the tune is not known, and there is uncertainty as to whether the words appeared first in the play or in the collection of songs, where they were not identified with Farquhar or the play. Whichever the case, "Over the Hills and far away" is much more a part of the play than "Come Fair One, be kind," which is known to have been written specifically for it.[2]

Farquhar is said to have based the plot on his own recruiting experiences while on military duty in the market town of Shrewsbury, where his comedy takes place.[3] In the scene Captain Plume, the recruiting officer, and his sergeant, Kite, cozen two drunken rustics into enlisting. It opens with Kite singing the song's tenth verse, "Our 'Prentice Tom;" the two prospects join in the refrain; a short while later the Captain makes his entrance also singing the air; and as the scene ends they all exit singing it in chorus.

The Recruiting Officer enjoyed tremendous popularity in the colonies throughout the century. Very likely it was given at Williamsburg's first theatre a dozen years or so after the initial London performance; it may have been one of the unidentified plays that William Byrd II attended there during the spring of 1721.[4]

The earliest documented performance of the play took place on December 6, 1732 in New York. Four years later in 1736 "the Gentlemen and Ladies of this Country" performed the comedy in Williamsburg. It was given in Norfolk in 1751 and almost certainly in Williamsburg by the Murray-Kean troupe during that company's final appearances in Virginia.[5]

The comedy was among the twenty-five plays that the Hallam Company had rehearsed in England before they came to Virginia in 1752, and can be traced in almost every acting season and circuit for the remainder of the colonial period. George Washington, whose diary attests that he rarely missed an opportunity to see a play, recorded attending a performance in 1771 in Dumfries, one of Virginia's theatre towns on the route between Williamsburg and Annapolis.[6]

The play was well liked by the Masons and, as could be expected, by the military. It also was a favorite vehicle for the talents of amateur groups such as the performers in Williamsburg in 1736. An amateur group of British officers stationed at Albany, New York, during the French and Indian War gave *The Recruiting Officer*, as well as another popular Farquhar play, *The Beaux' Stratagem*, in a fitted-up barn.[7]

After 1759 Lewis Hallam, Jr., played the role of Captain Plume in the colonies. Undoubtedly his father had played the part earlier. His stepfather, David Douglass, who had married his widowed mother in Jamaica, played Sergeant Kite—except in a 1773 performance in New York when the young Irish actor John Henry took the role.[8] The two country recruits were played at various times by Tomlinson, Allyn, Harman, Wall, Roberts, and Byerley, all of whom appeared in at least a few singing roles.

The song "Over the Hills and far away" was as popular in its own right as was the play. Its tune was often appropriated for verses on topical events, especially of political or martial import. At the time of the Scottish uprising in support of Bonnie Prince Charlie in 1745 a wave of patriotism swept through the theatres. It produced, among other songs, "God save the King" as well as a new set of words to the tune of "Over the Hills." The verses began "The Rebell Clans, in search of Prey/ come over the Hills and far away," and proclaimed "Great GEORGE shall Britons Scepter sway/And chace Rebellion far away."[9]

The tune was heard in another play as popular in the colonies as it was elsewhere, Gay's *The Beggar's Opera.* It is Air 16 in Act I, sung by Captain Macheath, the highwayman, and his new bride, Polly. Other ballad operas besides Gay's used the tune. It appeared in the 1731 edition of *The Devil to Pay*, and was one of the airs in *The Fashionable Lady*, the work of an expatriate Philadelphian, James Ralph, who had arrived in London at twenty-five accompanied by eighteen-year-old Benjamin Franklin.[10]

The song's persuasive refrain eventually skipped over the hills into the nursery song as the only tune that Tom the Piper's Son could play.[11]

[10]

'Tis True, My Good Dear

sung in

THE MOCK DOCTOR, or THE DUMB LADY CUR'D

A Ballad Opera by Henry Fielding

Henry Fielding (1707–1754) *Mr. Seedo (d. 1754)*

(**Moderately**)

'Tis true, my good Dear, I am Bone— of your Bone, Thank the Parson, Thank the Parson who stitch'd two Wretch-es in one, Who stitch'd two Wret-ches in one.

IN the opening scene of *The Mock Doctor*, the squire remonstrates with Gregory, the woodcutter, for beating his wife, Dorcas. Instead of being grateful, Dorcas tells the squire that their quarrel is none of his business, and bids him "go beat your own Rib, Sir, at home." Whereupon Gregory asks his wife to be friends again. Dorcas answers that she'll pardon him, but he'll pay for it, and sings this song.

"'Tis true, my good Dear" was the first of the three songs that Mr. Seedo, the music director at Drury Lane, composed in 1732 especially for Fielding's comedy, the third most popular of his ballad farces.[1] The other six songs were selected for the play from tunes in common currency.

The arrangement that Fielding, Coffey, and several other ballad writers had with Seedo to set original music to some of their lyrics was a departure from the custom of selecting airs from existing music of contemporary composers or from traditional tunes. Seedo also provided music for Fielding's *The Lottery* and for the revised version of his *The Author's Farce*, in which the author has him appear on stage in person as composer of the overture in the third act puppet show. Seedo left England in 1736 to direct the royal band at Potsdam, his departure hastened, perhaps, by the imminent licensing act and the rise of Thomas Arne as a favorite composer at the theatres.[2]

"The Farce taken from Moliere by Henry Fielding call'd *The Mock Doctor*"[3] was an established afterpiece in the colonies before the Hallam Company brought it to Virginia in their play stock in 1752, and remained so until its last recorded performance in 1769.[4] The pert Dorcas, who sings most of the songs and whose trick in paying her husband back provides the action in the play, was performed originally by Miss Raftor, the later Mrs. Clive. In the colonies the first Mrs. Owen Morris, until her accidental death by drowning in 1767, usually had the role, although Miss Wainwright had played it in Charleston in 1766, when she was billed as "Dorcas with the Songs in Character."[5]

[11]

Let's Have a Dance upon the Heath

sung in

MACBETH

Adapted from the Tragedy by William Shakespeare

[?] *Thomas Middleton (1570–1627),*
adapted by Sir William Davenant (1606–1668)

Attributed to Richard Leveridge (1670–1758)

which we dance in some_ old Mill up - on the hop - per Stone or_ Wheel, to
some old Saw or bard - ish Rhime, when still_ the Mill-clack does_ keep Time, when
still_ the Mill-clack does_ keep Time.
Some-times a - bout a

hol - low Tree, a - round, a - round, a - round dance we, And thi-ther the chirp - ing
Cric-kets come, And Bee - tles sing— in drow - sy Hum. Some-times we dance on
Fens— or Furze to Howl of Wolves or Barks of— Curs; Or if with none of
these we meet, we dance to the Ec - hoes of— our Feet
(Dance)

WHEN the reorganized Hallam Company began its tour of Maryland and Virginia in the spring of 1760, one of its stock plays was the perennial favorite of the eighteenth-century stage, the musically embellished version of *Macbeth*. The preceding winter, under the direction of David Douglass, the company had given performances of the tragedy in Philadelphia, where they advertised it in the *Pennsylvania Gazette* of October 25 as "Macbeth. Written by Shakespear. With the Whole Original Musick as set by PURCELL; Witches Dances and all the Decorations proper to the Play."

This billing of "Original Musick" (of which this song is a part), witches' dances, and decorations conformed to a long established pattern of advertisements for the play. But the Philadelphia notice contained one interesting exception to the pattern: the attribution of the "Whole Original Musick" to Purcell.

The question of the identity of the composer of this *Macbeth* music has been a problem for many years for musicologists interested in the eighteenth-century theatre. The name of Henry Purcell, the great Restoration musician, was not linked with the music in a printed edition until 1785, a quarter of a century after the colonial company's attribution. Dr. William Boyce, the eminent composer and organist, was the first to publish the *Macbeth* score in 1770, where he attributed it to another Restoration musician, Matthew Locke, although other composers in addition to Locke were known to have set songs for *Macbeth*, including John Eccles, Daniel Purcell, and the great basso and prolific song writer, Richard Leveridge. The evidence now points to Leveridge as the composer of this music.[1]

Macbeth was advertised to be performed at Drury Lane on November 21, 1702, "with the Vocal and Instrumental Musick, all new compos'd by Mr. Leveridge, and perform'd by him and others." In the many notices over the years that followed, his name was last mentioned as the composer on April 13, 1716; however, he continued to head the list of those who had the vocal parts in the musical portions of *Macbeth* until he quit the stage at eighty years of age.[2]

Leveridge's connection with *Macbeth* should have been familiar to the Hallams in the American Company. Several of the elder members of the family had appeared in the tragedy at Covent Garden in 1738 with Leveridge in his usual vocal part.[3]

The *Macbeth* songs, which were borrowed from Middleton's tragicomedy *The Witch* of 1610, are part of the incantations with which the witches invoke their noxious spells. Despite MacDuff's description of their singing as "hellish," the mood of the music is neither weird nor foreboding. Audiences took for granted that witches—popular in this and other contemporary plays—would be happy in successfully accomplishing their malevolent designs.[4]

In the colonial theatre the casting of Hecate, goddess of sorcery, and her subject witches varied from season to season, probably according to the make-up of the company. Three men played the witches in 1759, three women in 1767, and seven women in 1768. Both Catherine Maria Harman and her husband appeared in early performances of *Macbeth* in Philadelphia, he as one of the witches and she in the role of Hecate, to whom the song "Let's have a dance" was assigned. It was heard in the scene in Act II wherein the cabalistic crew confront MacDuff and his wife on the heath. After 1767 Stephen Woolls took over the part of Hecate, singing the music very effectively.[5]

The tune to "Let's have a dance" was familiar to colonial audiences from another play. It had been taken for Air 8 in Coffey's ballad opera of 1731, *The Devil to Pay*. Appropriately, the conjuring doctor in that work sang it to summon his little spirits to work their charms on the cobbler's wife and Lady Loverule. In the text the music is specified as "The Spirit's Song in Macbeth," and the music printed with the play in 1732 was the same as that issued nearly forty years later when Boyce published the Macbeth score.[6]

[12]

Ye Gods, Ye Gave to Me a Wife

sung in

THE DEVIL TO PAY, or THE WIVES METAMORPHOS'D

A Ballad Opera by Charles Coffey and Others

Unidentified *Mr. Seedo (d. 1754)*

[**Allegro non troppo**]

f *f*

Ye Gods! Ye gave to— me a Wife, out of your Grace and

6 6 6

Fa - vour, To be— the— Com - fort— of my Life, to— be— the— Com - fort—

6

of my Life, And I was glad to have her, But if your Pro - vi -
dence Di - vine for some-thing else de - sign_ her, To o - bey_ your Will at_
a - ny time, To o - bey_ your_ Will_ at_ a - ny time, I'm
rea - dy I'm rea - dy to_ re - sign_ her.

AMONG the ballad afterpieces composed "in the manner of *The Beggar's Opera*," the most successful and influential was *The Devil to Pay*. Its popularity lasted into the nineteenth century and encompassed the English provinces, the colonies, and the European continent. Translated and imitated in France, Italy, and Germany, where it affected the development of the *Singspiel*, the farce played an important part in the history of comic opera.[1]

Considerably more than the recorded thirty-odd colonial performances are implied in the appearance of the afterpiece on every circuit and in every season from 1736 until the Revolution. Williamsburg must have seen the Murray-Kean production of *The Devil to Pay* before the Hallams arrived with it in their stock of plays.[2]

The one-act version of the ballad farce was a patchwork by several authors. Charles Coffey and John Mottley, two unsuccessful playwrights, collaborated in adapting *The Devil to Pay* from a comedy by Thomas Jevon, a seventeenth-century dancing master and actor. First produced in three acts at Drury Lane in August 1731, it was not successful until Theophilus Cibber tailored it to one act two months later.[3] Theophilus, the actor son of Colley Cibber, was satirized with his father in Henry Fielding's *The Author's Farce* as "a couple of poetical Tailors" who cut a play as a tailor does his coat.[4]

Of the sixteen songs that remained after the tailoring, Sir John's air, "Ye Gods, ye gave to me a Wife," is noted in the play text as "Set by Mr. Seedo." Seedo, a musician and composer active in London theatres from 1723 to 1736, was music director at Drury Lane in 1732. He wrote and arranged music for several ballad-opera authors including Coffey and Fielding. Thus he may have been in charge of the music for *The Devil to Pay*.[5]

Seedo's song in *The Devil to Pay* is the first of three sung by "the honest Country Gentleman," Sir John Loverule, in the scene in which his second wife, "a proud, canting, brawling, fanatical Shrew," breaks up a party in the servants' hall and a violin over the fiddler's head.[6] At the conclusion of this song, Sir John observes, "Thus it is to be marry'd to a continual Tempest." When his lady drives away a "Doctor of Astrology and Physick" who sought shelter for the night, Sir John, who has been "belov'd for his Hospitality," petitions in his third song, which closes the scene, that his wife be conveyed to "some distant Shore, Where I may ne'er behold her more."

[13]

The Early Horn

sung in

THE DEVIL TO PAY, or THE WIVES METAMORPHOS'D

A Ballad Opera by Charles Coffey and Others

Edward Phillips (fl. 1730–1740) *John Ernest Galliard (1680–1749)*

ear - ly Horn, sa - lute the Morn that gilds this charm - ing
Place. With chear - ful Cries bids Ec - ho rise, and
join the jo - vial Chase. and
join the jo - vial Chase, and

join the jo - vial Chase,
f
mp
With ear - ly Horn, sa - lute the Morn that
p
gilds the charm - ing Place. With chear - ful Cries bid
p
Ec - ho rise, bid Ec - ho rise, and
mp

join the jo - vial Chase.
mf
p
With chear - ful Cries bids Ec - ho rise, and

adagio
allegro
join the jo - vial Chase, And join the jo - vial Chase.
f
adagio
Fine

The vo - cal Hills a - round, The wav - ing Woods, the crys - tal floods,
all, all re - turn th'en-liv - ing Sound. The
vo - cal hills a - round, The wav - ing Woods, the crys - tal Floods
all, all re - turn th'en-liv - ing Sound.
D.C. al Fine

"THE EARLY HORN" became a permanent addition to *The Devil to Pay* after the famous tenor John Beard introduced it into the part of Sir John Loverule in the 1738–39 season at Drury Lane. Beard, former choir boy of the Chapel Royal, had first sung it at Covent Garden in 1736 as the opening number in *The Royal Chace, or Merlin's Cave*, with music by John Ernest Galliard, the oboist and composer. Galliard provided much music for the theatres, especially for the popular and elaborate pantomimes and masques of the period.[1]

The probable and appropriate place for the interpolation of the song in *The Devil to Pay* occurs at the beginning of the scene in which Sir John returns home from an early-morning hunt, unaware that the conjuring Doctor has "metamorphos'd" Lady Loverule and the gentle wife of Jobson, the cobbler, so that each has awakened in the home and guise of the other but with temperaments unchanged.

Before the spell is lifted, the churlish Jobson has discovered what it is to have a shrewish wife, and Lady Loverule has been effectively cured of her rancor by the cobbler, who expresses his philosophy in a song that concludes the farce: "There's naught but the Devil and this good Strap could ever tame a Scold."

Playbills both in England and in America frequently featured the song in association with the role of Sir John, who also had five other songs: three solos, a "duetto" dialogue with Nell, and the concluding trio with Jobson and Lady Loverule. In the American Company's casts Stephen Woolls consistently was listed as "Sir John, in which Character he will sing 'The Early Horn'." The first Sir John Loverule in London had been Michael Stoppelaer, an actor and tenor who sang for Handel. In the colonies the first to play the role of Sir John was William Adcock, the singing actor in the Hallam Company's first seasons.[2]

The farce was the last musical afterpiece to be performed in the colonies before the Revolution.[3]

[14]

Sabina with an Angel's Face

sung in

THE CARELESS HUSBAND
A Comedy by Colley Cibber

Colley Cibber (1671–1757) *Daniel Purcell (ca. 1660–1717)*

(poco rit)
(somewhat faster)
And then des - troy.
With all the Arts of Look and
Dress, She fans the fa - - tal Fire. Thro'
Pride mis - ta-ken oft for Grace, She bids the Swain ex - pire. Thro'

Pride mis - ta - ken oft for Grace, She bids the Swain, She
bids the Swain ex - - pire
(moderately)
f
f
The God of Love en - rag'd, The God of Love en - rag'd to see the
tr
mf
Nymph de - fy his Flame, pro - nounc'd this mer - ci - less De - cree a - gainst the

haugh - - ty Dame, pro - nounc'd this mer - ci-less De- cree a - gainst the
(a little faster)
haugh - - ty Dame: Let Age with dou - ble Speed o'er - take her, Let
Love the Room of Pride sup-ply; And when her Lov - ers all for -
sake her, Let her then, then, then, let her then un - pi - tied die! And

THE intrigues of a neglectful husband, Sir Charles Easy, and the discords of the love affair between Lady Betty Modish and Lord Lovemore furnished the plot and subplot for Cibber's play, first performed at Drury Lane in 1704. After the author resolved the complications, through repentance on the part of the philandering husband and reconciliation of the lovers, he ended his comedy with an entertainment, of which this song was a part. Authors often used the device to introduce music into their plays.[1]

Cibber, who liked to sing and loved music and the opera, regularly provided for incidental music in his plays.[2] In *The Careless Husband* he had a servant announce to the assembled company in the final scene that "Mr. LeFevre and the Musick" (i.e., the musicians) were below, desiring to know what time it would please to have them begin. This song was sung at the end of their entertainment. The text was printed in the play and, as stated on the single-sheet copy of the music, was sung by the noted professional theatre singer and composer, Richard Leveridge, who must have assumed the character of LeFevre or of one of the "Musick." The name LeFevre is close enough to Leveridge to suggest a private joke on the part of Cibber, or one of the innumerable puns to which Daniel Purcell, the composer, was addicted.[3]

Neither Leveridge nor the role of LeFevre was listed in the casts of characters, but most of the early notices of the play mentioned "Singing by Leveridge." Similarly, in a New York performance of the comedy in 1753, the Hallam Company's featured singer, William Adcock, was not listed in the cast, but was billed as singing. Probably this was a repeat performance of the play from the Williamsburg season of the preceding year, since *The Careless Husband* was among the rehearsed plays that the Hallams are known to have brought to Virginia.[4]

A copy of the words of "Sabina with an Angel's Face" was found among the manuscripts of William Byrd of Westover. Byrd, who was a frequent theatregoer during his long residence in London, undoubtedly heard Leveridge sing this song in the play. While in London in 1718, Byrd patronized the coffee house that Leveridge owned and attended plays in which Leveridge appeared.[5]

[15]

Indiana's Song

sung in

THE CONSCIOUS LOVERS

A Play by Sir Richard Steele

Sir Richard Steele (1672–1729) *Attributed to John Ernest Galliard (1680–1749)*

2

My inward Pang, my secret Grief,
My soft consenting Looks betray;
He loves, but gives me no Relief—
Why speaks not he who may?

SIR RICHARD STEELE, one of the most important literary figures of the early eighteenth-century, wrote the text to this song as an expression of the plight of Indiana, the much-afflicted heroine of his play. Orphaned, shipwrecked, and penniless, Indiana has been rescued from a designing guardian by Bevil, with whom she has fallen in love. Bevil, betrothed to another, is too honorable to reveal his own feelings.

Steele intended the song, "the distress of a lovesick maid," to be sung as an entertainment for Indiana. It was to come at the end of the scene in Act II in which she complained to Bevil that the Italian operas then being given in London didn't permit the mind to share in the entertainment.[1]

The song was omitted from the first production of *The Conscious Lovers* in 1722. In the preface to the published edition—in which the song text was printed—Steele explained that he "revives here a Song which was omitted for want of a Performer. Signor Carbonelli instead of it played on the Fiddle. . . ." Stefano Carbonelli was the conductor of the operas discussed by Indiana. He was introduced in person to play a violin solo.[2]

Successfully reinstated in the play, the song was often featured in Act II in the theatre bills and was set by several composers during the eighteenth century. The setting used here, printed in *The Musical Miscellany* in 1729 as "Sung in the Conscious Lovers," is considered to be that by John Ernest Galliard, oboist and noted theatre composer. Steele mentioned him in connection with the song, published without music in his periodical *The Theatre*, while *The Conscious Lovers*, his last and most important play, was still in preparation. He titled it "The Love Sick Maid. A Song set by Mr. Galliard."[3]

Vocalists featured in London bills as singing in Act II included Thomas Lowe, a noted tenor, whom William Beverley, a Virginia burgess and councillor, heard at a performance of the play at Covent Garden in October 1750.[4]

When the Hallam Company arrived in Virginia in 1752 they had Steele's play in their repertoire. Music was mentioned for the first time in connection with a colonial performance of the play at the beginning of the Hallam Company's first New York season in 1753. Philip Schuyler, a twenty-year-old native of Albany, wrote a friend that "a sprightly young man named Hulett played the violin and danced merrily" at the performance Schuyler attended of *The Conscious Lovers*.[5]

William Hulett, "late apprentice to Mr. Grenier of the City of London," in addition to providing the entertainment between the acts, possibly furnished music for Act II. However, Mrs. Love, a featured singer with the company, probably was the entertainer of Indiana.[6]

[16]

Love's a Sweet and Soft Musician

sung in

THE MUSICAL LADY

A Comedy by George Colman the Elder

George Colman (1732–1794) | *Unidentified*

thee; Plays on ev' - - - - ry Dis - po - si - - tion, Strikes the
Soul on ev'-ry Key. Deep Dis-pair now thrums A - da - gio, Live-ly
Hope now sounds Cor-ra - gio; Oh, the ra - - vish-ing trans- i - - tion, Twee-dle
Dum and Twee-dle Dee.
mf

WILLIAMSBURG playgoers who heeded the announcement in the *Virginia Gazette* of October 17, 1771, that "on Wednesday next the Theatre in the City will be opened with the Comedy of *The West Indian*, and *The Musical Lady*" would have heard Sophy sing this song during her music lesson with Signor Rosini in Act I, scene 2 of the afterpiece.[1]

Colman's comedy was fashioned in 1762 from the portion that he and David Garrick had pruned from Colman's *The Jealous Wife*, a comedy given in Williamsburg later in the 1771 season. Although neither Colman nor his friend and rival theatre manager, Garrick, had an ear for music, both provided it in quantity and quality to fit the expectations of their patrons.[2]

Colman's afterpiece, which satirized the music of Italian opera in England and the affectations of some of its sponsors, presupposed a familiarity on the part of the audience with the subject of the ridicule. The script, full of musical terms and allusions, calls for several songs and a number of musical instruments as props, including an armonica.[3]

Sophy calls this song a "little Venetian ballad tune" and sings it to the accompaniment her music teacher plays on the "viol-di gambo." Her suitor, Mask, who pretends a devotion equal to her own pose of infatuation for Italian music, has supposedly written the words. The ending comes from the famous "Epigram on the Feuds between Handel and Bononcini," verses written by John Byrom in 1725: "Strange all this Difference should be/'Twixt Tweedle-dum and Tweedle-dee!" and refers to the quarrel between the factions involved with Italian opera in London.[4]

In Act II Sophy sings a second song, "Fonte Amiche."[5] A third song, a burlesque trio, was sung on the English stage by well-known professional theatre singers. According to the play text, the trio was set by Jonathan Battishill, the composer-harpsichordist at Covent Garden; he may also have arranged the rest of the music.

Jane Pope, the twenty-year-old actress daughter of a barber and wigmaker to the theatre, played Sophy at the first Drury Lane performance in 1762. A singing actress cast as Sophy at Covent Garden in 1767 was Mrs. Mattocks, the former Isabella Hallam. She was the youngest daughter of the Lewis Hallams of the colonial company, who had left her in England when they went to Virginia in 1752. Her cousin, the extravagantly admired singer and actress Nancy Hallam, played Sophy in the colonies. David Benjamin Roberts, a singing actor with the American Company, played Rosini, the English music master whom Mask had bribed to teach Sophy under an Italian name, obviously chosen by Colman from the rosin used for violin bows.[6]

The Musical Lady was acted for the first time in America in April 1769, at the "particular Desire of the Grand Knot of the Friendly Brothers of St. Patrick." Two months later the play was read at the Assembly Room in Philadelphia and "the Songs sung."[7] Sophy's first song was preserved apart from the play both in single-sheet form and in the pages of the *London Magazine* for November 1773, where it was available to colonial subscribers.[8]

{17}

Water Parted from the Sea

sung in

ARTAXERXES

Translated from the Opera Libretto by Pietro Metastasio

Pietro Metastasio (1698–1782); translated by Thomas A. Arne — *Thomas A. Arne (1710–1778)*

mp
tr
Wa - - ter part - - ed from the Sea,
(tr)
p
tr
May in - crease the Ri - - ver's Tide,
To the bub - - ling Fount' may flee,
(tr)
(tr)

tr
O'er the fer - - tile Val - - leys glide.
tr
tr
tr tr
Tho' in the Search of lost Re - pose,
tr
tr

Thro' the Land 'tis free to roam,
Still it mur - murs as it flows,
pant - ing for its na - tive Home.
Tho' in Search of lost Re - pose,

Thro' the Land 'tis free to roam,
Still it murmurs as it flows,
Pant - ing for its na - tive Home.

AMONG the most popular and widely known theatre songs in America in the second half of the eighteenth century were the airs from Dr. Arne's *Artaxerxes*. Arne, experimenting with opera in English in the style of the Italian *opera seria*, in 1762 composed the music to his own translation of the *Artaserse* of Pietro Metastasio. His translation gave Samuel Foote the opportunity to satirize Arne as "Dr. Catgut," the singing master turned poet, in his comedy *The Commissary* in 1764.[1]

Although the opera was not given in this country until the nineteenth century, the songs from it were performed in concert halls, in pleasure gardens, and between acts at the theatres, and were practiced, referred to, and copied into manuscript music books.[2]

Arne's former pupil Stephen Woolls made his New York debut at an entertainment there on July 15, 1767, singing "Water parted from the Sea" and another song from *Artaxerxes*, "Thou like the glorious Sun." Woolls, whose singing was a feature of the playbills even when no cast was printed, undoubtedly sang them in other cities on the colonial circuit, including Williamsburg.[3]

There is evidence that some Virginians were familiar with the song. For example, on December 22, 1773, at one of the Carter family's many musical evenings at Nomini Hall in Virginia's Northern Neck, Philip Fithian, the tutor, recorded that Councilor Robert Carter played "Water parted from the Sea" on the armonica. Carter, an ardent devotee of music, kept a collection of instruments at Nomini Hall and an organ in his home in Williamsburg.[4] The following March Carter, who often occupied himself transposing music, wrote out for his daughter Nancy the music to "Infancy," another air from the opera, which she was "to get by Heart & sing it with the *Guitar*."[5]

"Water parted from the Sea sung by Arbaces in the celebrated Opera *Artaxerxes*, sung by Sign. Tenducci," was the title under which the song was copied into one of the manuscript books in which Robert Bolling, burgess from Buckingham County, Virginia, and his son Linnaeus accumulated the music that pleased them. The accompaniment was arranged for two guitars and signed "B.ll..g."[6]

[18]

Castalio's Complaint

sung in

THE ORPHAN, or THE UNHAPPY MARRIAGE

A Tragedy by Thomas Otway

Thomas Otway (*1652–1685*) | *William Boyce* (*1710–1779*)

Head, Let none his Sor - rows hide. But Hand in
Hand, A - round me move, Sing - ing the sad - dest
Tales of Love; And see, when your Com - plaints ye join, If
all your Wrongs, if all your Wrongs can e - qual mine.

2

The happiest Mortal once was I,
My Heart no Sorrow knew.
Pity the Pain of which I die,
But ask not whence it grew.
Yet if a tempting Fair you find,
That's very lovely, very kind,
Tho' bright as Heaven, whose Stamp she bears,
Think on my Fate, and shun her Snares.

THE tragedy "wrote by the ingenuous Mr. Otway," as a New York playbill put it in 1750, centers on the fateful love that Castalio and his twin brother, Polydore, bear for their father's ward, Monimia.[1] Unaware that Castalio has won Monimia and secretly married her, the jealous Polydore overhears them plan what he thinks is an illicit rendezvous. Pretending to be Castalio, Polydore keeps his brother's appointment in Monimia's chamber, from which Castalio, arriving too late, is barred. When the truth is known, it brings death to all three.

Act V opens with the despondent Castalio lying on the ground in the garden. The song—almost certainly intended to be sung off stage, whence its echoing of his grief served as an effective theatrical device to intensify the mood of the tragedy—could have been sung by Castalio himself if a professional theatre singer were not available.

Castalio was played in New York by John Henry and in Williamsburg by William Verling. Henry, whose roles were frequently billed with songs, joined the American Company in 1767 from the theatre in Jamaica; he was described as being "of more than respectable musical acquirement." Verling, also recorded in singing roles, made his first appearance on the colonial stage with the American Company in Charleston in 1766.[2]

The Orphan was a stock piece in British theatrical companies, and the colonial ones were no exception. A verse epilogue which was provided for the first recorded performance in Charleston in 1735 described the play as "one of the choicest Treasures of the Old World to regale the New" and mentioned the "powerful music" which tuned "its warbling throat." From then until 1774 the tragedy was acted throughout the colonies. Two performances were recorded in Boston, which usually frowned on dramatic entertainment.[3]

The play was also available in print. The *Virginia Gazette* advertised Otway's plays in two volumes (first published in 1713); the Byrd library at Westover contained two volumes; and Thomas Jefferson owned a three-volume collection of Otway's *Works* published in 1768, which included the plays.[4]

Castalio's song was as durable as the play. By the time the Hallam Company arrived in Virginia in 1752, the song had been provided with four different settings. If the play was among those given in Williamsburg's first theatre, the first of these would have been heard in it, that by Francis Forcer (1650–1705), a seventeenth-century theatre composer and the co-owner of the music house and garden at Sadler's Wells. Two anonymous settings appeared in the eighteenth century before a fourth was made by the respected church and theatre musician William Boyce. Boyce's setting appeared in two song collections, as well as in the *London Magazine* for April 1752, where it was obtainable in the colonies.[5]

{19}

The Life of a Beau

sung in

THE MISER

A Comedy by Henry Fielding

James Miller (1706–1744) | *Henry Carey (ca. 1687–1743)*

2

For Nothing they rise but to draw the fresh Air,
Spend the Morning in Nothing but curling their Hair,
And do Nothing all Day but sing, saunter, and stare,
Such, such is the Life . . . etc.

3

For Nothing at Night to the Playhouse they crowd,
For to mind Nothing done there they always are proud,
But to bow, and to grin and talking—Nothing aloud,
Such, such is the Life . . . etc.

4

For Nothing they run to th'Assembly and Ball,
And for Nothing at Cards a fair Partner call,
For they still must be beasted* who've—Nothing at all,
Such, such is the Life . . . etc.

5

For Nothing on Sundays at Church they appear,
For they've Nothing to hope nor they've Nothing to fear,
They can be Nothing nowhere who—Nothing are here,
Such, such is the Life . . . etc.

*A penalty at cards, especially ombre and quadrille.

THE MISER, a comedy that Fielding refashioned in 1733 from Molière's *L'Avare*, was performed in Williamsburg on June 8, 1768, the playbill calling particular notice to the appearance of Mrs. Osborne as Lappet, maid to the miser's daughter. No doubt the colonial company hoped that the lively Henrietta Osborne would prove to be as popular in the role as had its London originator, the famous Kitty Clive. Fielding himself could well have been pleased by the playbill's emphasis, as he had designed the first three scenes to enhance the part for Catherine Raftor, soon to become Mrs. Clive.[1]

There was no song for Lappet in Fielding's text. However the playbill for a Drury Lane performance on September 15, 1739, announced Mrs. Clive as Lappet with a song, "The Life of a Beau," taken from the "Farce of the Coffee House." It was one of three songs composed by Henry Carey for the Reverend James Miller's "new Dramatick Piece intermix'd with Songs in Character," given on January 26, 1738, at Drury Lane with Mrs. Clive as Miss Kitty.[2]

Like "The Early Horn," introduced into *The Devil to Pay*, "The Life of a Beau" is another example of a song popular in one play permanently incorporated into another by its original performer in a new role. The song was featured in the bills with Mrs. Clive as the singer during the next quarter of a century, and was also introduced into another of her roles.[3]

Opinions varied about Mrs. Clive's vocal ability. Burney thought her singing was "intolerable when she meant it to be fine," but in ballad farces and songs of humor it "was like her comic acting, everything it should be." Handel cast her as Delilah in his oratorio *Samson* in 1743, having earlier set two theatre songs for her, and her way with a song was such that her singing roles were repeatedly featured in the theatre bills.[4]

At least a minimum proficiency in singing was expected of the eighteenth-century thespians, particularly those who played leading roles. Mrs. Clive, in a complaint about her contract in 1744, wrote that she had been at great expense in paying "Masters for singing over which Article alone Managers now give £6 a week." According to Burney, her music master was Henry Carey, who composed, "The Life of a Beau," which, with other of his theatre songs, she helped popularize.[5]

It is not known where in the play Lappet sang "The Life of a Beau," but in the opening scene between her and Ramillie, the manservant, there is an amusing reference to their mutual interest in music. Ramillie, who prefers it to everything but the ladies, offers to steal his master's silver ticket so that Lappet may attend the opera of *Cato*,[6] remarking, "I know he is engaged tomorrow with some Gentlemen who never leave their Bottle for Musick." To this Lappet replies, "Ah, the Savages!" and may have continued with her musical comment on the beaux.

Henrietta Osborne, the Lappet of the Virginia Company of Comedians, the newly organized rival to the established American Company, had made her colonial debut with the latter group in Charleston during the season of 1765–66 as one of the new performers whom David Douglass, the manager, had recruited in England. Although she appeared in singing roles, her dancing was usually a feature of the bills. From the coincidence of dates it would appear that she was the Miss Osborne, "a young lady from Jamaica," who made her first appearance at Drury Lane on October 8, 1759. Alexander Purdie's *Virginia Gazette* of February 4, 1768 reprinted on request the prologue that Mrs. Osborne had spoken the month before on her benefit night in Norfolk, in which she recalled "ten long years this motley life I've led."[7]

[20]

Ballynamony

sung in

THE BRAVE IRISHMAN, or CAPTAIN O'BLUNDER

A Comedy by Thomas Sheridan

Thomas Sheridan (1719–1788) | *Unidentified*

2

Since the first Time I saw you, I take no repose,
I sleep all the Day to forget half my Woes;
So strong is the Flame in my Bosom that glows,
By St. Patrick, I fear it will burn thro' my Cloaths.
Ballynamony, ho, ro, etc.

3

By my Soul, I'm afraid I shall die in my Grave
Unless you'll comply, and poor Phelim will save;
Then grant the Petition your Lover doth crave,
Who never was free till you made him your Slave.
Ballynamony, ho, ro, etc.

4

On that happy Day when I make you my Bride,
With a swinging long Sword, how I'll strut and I'll stride!
In a Coach and six Horses with my Honey I'll ride,
As before you I walk to the Church by your side.
Ballynamony, ho, ro, etc.

CAPTAIN O'BLUNDER, the loquaciously confused Irish hero of Thomas Sheridan's farcical afterpiece, brushes aside the confession of bankruptcy by Lucy's father. He announces his intention to make Lucy his bride and even to share his estate with her and her father. Then he gives them a song he "made upon this dear creature."

The words of this song in *The Brave Irishman* also are to be found in the printed text of *The Double Disappointment* by Moses Mendez. This "ballad opera," given at Drury Lane a month and a half after the first London performance of Sheridan's play in January 1746, was also one of the afterpieces in the colonial repertoire.[1] Mendez also borrowed O'Blunder's name for his fortune-hunting Irishman, who in his farce turns out to be a knave rather than a hero.

Single-sheet copies of the song issued from about 1747 through 1765 were printed with the title "Balin a mone" and usually with the additional notation: "as sung by Mr. Bar[r]ington in *The Double Disappointment*."[2] The Mendez version has an additional line in the refrain to enhance the comical effect which is also stressed by the music:

1. A Kiss of your sweet Lips for me.
2. Your pretty black Hair for me.
3. Your pretty black Eyes for me.
4. Your lilly white Fist for me.

The first London performance of the comedy took place at the Hallam's theatre in Goodman's Fields on January 31, 1746. As an afterpiece to *Hamlet*, it was announced as "never perform'd there before, wrote by Mr. Sheridan the player." Schemewell was played by Lewis Hallam, who brought his acting company to Virginia several years later. The only other member of the cast mentioned was Banberry, who played O'Blunder.[3]

Sheridan, an actor-manager in Dublin who also appeared on the English stage, was said to have written the first version of *The Brave Irishman* while an undergraduate at Trinity College, Dublin, from which he received a bachelor of arts degree in 1739.[4] He was the son of Dr. Thomas Sheridan, the "very eminent" schoolmaster and scholar of languages, whose death was noted in the *Virginia Gazette* of January 2, 1738. The junior Sheridan married Frances Chamberlaine, also a playwright, in 1747. Their son, Richard Brinsley Sheridan (1751–1816), became a noted dramatist.

John Henry, the Irish actor who joined the American Company while still in his early twenties, is said to have made his stage debut under the patronage of Thomas Sheridan. In the New York performance of *The Brave Irishman* on May 9, 1768, Henry played the title role.[5]

The farce was given everywhere on the colonial circuit after 1765, with a few performances reported after the Revolution. An extant Williamsburg playbill of the Virginia Company of Comedians for a performance of the farce as the afterpiece to *The Miser* on June 8, 1768, lists Mr. Farrell as "Capt. O'Blunder with a Song." He probably was the "Mr. Furell" who first appeared as a singing actor with the American Company in Charleston on March 26, 1764. In 1769, when the Virginia troupe appeared in Annapolis as the New American Company, William Verling played the role.[6]

As might be expected, a New York performance on March 17, 1769, was attended by the Grand Knot of the Friendly Sons of St. Patrick.[7]

[21]

Farewell, Ungrateful Traytor

sung in

THE SPANISH FRIAR, or THE DOUBLE DISCOVERY
A Tragicomedy by John Dryden

John Dryden (1631–1700) *Simon Pack (fl. 1678–1702)*

2

'Tis easie to deceive us,
In Pity of your Pain;
But when we love, you leave us
To rail at you in vain;
Before we have descry'd it,
There is no Bliss beside it;
But she that once has try'd it
Will never love again.

3

The Passion you pretended
Was only to obtain;
But when the Charm is ended,
The Charmer you disdain;
Your Love by ours we measure,
'Til we have lost our Treasure;
But dying is a Pleasure
When living is a Pain.

LEONORA, queen of Aragon, disturbed by the unexplained agitation of her bridegroom, Torrismond, is reassured by her maid Teresa. However, her "heavy heart forebodes some ill at hand," and she asks Teresa to "soothe my sadness" by singing "the song which poor Olympia made when false Bireno left her."[1] The song was heard in the opening scene of Act V of the tragicomedy, whose title was taken from its comic sub-plot. At the first performance, at Dorset Garden Theatre in 1680 when "all the world" was at the new play, Teresa was played by Mrs. Crofts.[2]

John Dryden, then poet laureate, wrote the play five years before Charles II's death in 1685. That it met with subsequent royal disapproval is shown in an eighteenth-century memoir. This relates that Queen Mary, daughter of James II, in 1689, the year after her father's dethronement and Dryden's loss of his laureateship, "gave herself the diversion of a play." Her unfortunate choice was *The Spanish Friar*, which "put her in some disorder." It was "the only play forbid by the late King."[3]

Captain Simon Pack, who set Dryden's song text, was a professional military man whose avocation was music. Between 1680 and 1694 he composed songs for at least eight plays, besides other music published in the songbooks and collections of the period. "Farewell ungrateful Traytor" was published in all editions of *Pills to Purge Melancholy* from 1706 to 1719. The tune also was used as a broadside ballad air.[4]

The Spanish Friar was performed in the colonies from 1735, or perhaps earlier at Williamsburg's first theatre, until 1769. The only known cast is from a Hallam Company performance in New York in 1753, when Teresa was played by Miss Hallam, who appeared with the company only that season. She has been identified as Lewis Hallam's elder daughter, for whom and her two brothers, Adam and Lewis, Jr., benefit performances were given in the spring of 1754. However, Philip Schuyler, who attended a performance of *The Conscious Lovers* the same season, referred to her in a letter as the sister of Lewis Hallam, Sr.[5]

Other plays of Dryden's seen on the colonial stage were *Amphitryon* and two adaptations of Shakespeare, *All for Love* and *The Tempest.* His *Alexander's Feast,* to which Handel set music, was in Robert Carter's library at Nomini Hall, and his plays were in other colonial libraries.[6]

[22]

Dirge

sung in

CYMBELINE

A Play by William Shakespeare

William Collins (1721–1759) — *Thomas A. Arne (1710–1778)*

2

[*p*] The Redbreast oft' at Ev'ning hours,
Shall kindly lend his little aid,
With hoary Moss and gather'd Flow'rs
To deck the Ground where thou art laid.

3

[*f*] When howling Winds and beating Rain
In tempest shake the sylvan Cell,
Or midst the Chace on ev'ry Plain,
The tender Thought on thee shall dwell.

4

Each lonely scene shall thee restore,
For thee the Tear be duly shed,
Belov'd 'till Life cou'd charm no more,
And mourn'd 'till Pity's self be dead.

A PAINTING that hangs today in the Raleigh Tavern in Williamsburg is a tangible and valued link to America's colonial theatre. It portrays Nancy Hallam in the role of Imogen in Shakespeare's *Cymbeline*. The painting shows her standing before the cave where Imogen, disguised as the youth Fidele, has taken refuge. It is the same cave before which, in a later scene, Arviragus (who turns out to be one of Imogen's long lost brothers) sings this dirge over the comatose form of the supposed Fidele.

The American-born artist Charles Willson Peale (1741–1827) painted the Hallam portrait between 1769, when he returned from his London studies, and November 1771, when a poem addressed to him, referring to the picture and complimenting its subject, was printed in the *Maryland Gazette*.[1]

Thomas Arne composed the music for Fidele's dirge to the text of William Collins, a poet who had won acclaim at seventeen for his *Persian Eclogues* and later for his pastoral poems. Collins's poem, which was printed in the *Gentleman's Magazine* for October 1749, had appeared the previous year with Arne's music in the composer's song collection, *Lyric Harmony*. At first as a solo, and later as a part song, it remained immensely popular, although Arne later made a setting of the original Shakespeare text.[2]

There were frequent revisions and alterations of the play during the eighteenth century. It was the Garrick alteration of 1761 that was announced for the first known colonial performances in 1767 in Philadelphia and New York.[3] The American Company kept the play in stock during its subsequent tours until it disbanded after the Charleston season of 1774. Williamsburg undoubtedly saw it during the Maryland-Virginia seasons of 1770–72.

Stephen Woolls, the company's much featured male vocalist, had the role of Arviragus "with a Song." Although Imogen at first was played by Margaret Cheer, the role later was taken over by the popular Miss Nancy Hallam. Her appearances in it at the Annapolis theatre drew extravagant praises for her talents and voice in the columns of the *Maryland Gazette*—both in poetry and in prose. She received homage throughout the colonies: in Charleston audiences anticipated "her developing genius"; in Philadelphia she won "universal Applause and Encouragement"; and theatre patrons in Williamsburg considered her "superfine."[4]

At least one of the poetical tributes must have been contributed by the Reverend Jonathan Boucher, rector of St. Ann's, Annapolis, and master of boys' schools in Caroline County, Virginia, and in Annapolis which were attended by George Washington's stepson, John Parke Custis. Boucher recalled in his memoirs that while at Annapolis he had written "some verses on one of the actresses and a prologue or two."[5]

[23]

Aileen Aroon

sung in

LOVE A-LA-MODE

A Comedy by Charles Macklin

[?] *Carrol O'Daly (fl. early 17th century)* | *Carrol O'Daly*

roon. Du-ca tu_ non_ van--na tu, Du-ca tu_ non_ van--na tu,
Du-ca tu, du-ca tu, du-ca tu_ non_ van-na_ tu, Oh,
Du-ca tu_ non_ van--na tu, Ai-leen A--roon.
(Ritornel solo)
mf
6

(Tutti)
mf
mp
Kead mil - - le Fal - - tie rote, Ai - leen A - - roon; Kead mil - - - le
Fal - - tie rote, Ai - leen A - - roon.
Kead mil - - le Fal - tie rote,
Shaet mil - le Fal - tie rote, Oet mil - - le, nee mil - - le, deh mil - le,

Fal - - tie rote, Oh,___ Fal - tie__ gus__ fine___ rote, Ai - leen A - roon.
(Ritornel solo)
mf
tr
(Tutti)
tr
tr
Tu-ca me a - ni

tr
an - - na me, sgra ma chree stu, O tu-ca me, a - ni an - - na me,
sgra ma chree stu. Tu-ca a - - ni an - - na me, tu - - ca me
an - - na me tu - - ca me, tu - - ca me tu-ca me sni, an - - na me,
Oh, Tu-ca me a - ni an - - na me, sgra me chree stu.
(rit.)

Will you come or will you stay, Aileen Aroon?*
A hundred thousand welcomes to you, Aileen Aroon.
Seven thousand, eight thousand,
Nine thousand, ten thousand
Welcomes to you,
One and twenty welcomes to you, Aileen Aroon.
I will come and I will not stay
For you are the love of my heart.

*i.e., Eileen, my dear.

BY particular desire," the young and charming Maria Storer sang "Ellin a Roon" in a performance of Charles Macklin's *Love a-la-Mode* on St. John's Day, June 24, 1773, at the John Street Theatre in New York with the Masons in attendance. She was not included in the cast that night, but eighteenth-century managers could usually find some plausible excuse to introduce a singer not called for in the script. In this instance Sir Callaghan O'Brallaghan's feigned reluctance to sing to his "bewitching Charlotte" the song called for in Act II may have provided the opportunity for introducing Maria Storer to sing "Ellin a Roon" in its place.[1]

Just ten days previously Miss Storer had sung the song as inter-act entertainment. Playbills for several preceding years, including one for a performance of this same afterpiece, had featured her singing between the acts. Virginians may have heard her sing "Ellin a Roon" in the 1771 and 1772 seasons, when *Love a-la-Mode* was given in Williamsburg and Fredericksburg. A playbill for the latter performance shows that it was the afterpiece to *The Provok'd Husband*, in which Maria Storer played Jennie, a role provided with two songs. She may have sung the Irish air between the acts or introduced it into the farce, as she did later in New York.[2]

It would appear that no eighteenth-century playgoer—Irish, English, or colonial—could have missed this song. Its popularity dated from 1742, when Kitty Clive returned from a season in Ireland and on March 8 at Drury Lane sang the song in Gaelic. Thereafter it was frequently performed on the stage by her and by others, including the mother of Maria Storer, who had begun her career as a singer in Handel's operas in Dublin in 1742. As a singing actress her billings frequently featured this song as well as Handel's arias. Maria, the youngest of her actress daughters, sang many of the same songs and played many of the same singing roles that had been in her mother's repertoire. After the Revolution, she was considered the finest public singer America had known.[3]

The music and original text of "Aileen Aroon" are attributed to Carrol O'Daly, a seventeenth-century Irish harper and poet. It is considered to be one of the earliest Irish harp tunes to which the appropriate words are extant. The song's popularity held to the end of the eighteenth century. "Allan Aroon," without the words and arranged for harpsichord, is in the manuscript music book that belonged to the wife of Thomas Jefferson, Martha Wayles Jefferson. "Ailun a'Roon, or Welcome My Ellun, an Old Irish Air," is in the *European Magazine* for 1794. The spellings of the title were as varied as the texts to which the tune was set. It finally lost its name altogether with the waxing nineteenth-century popularity of the version with which it is now associated, "Robin Adair."[4]

Removing the song from its time-honored position as an inter-act feature and interpolating it into *Love a-la-Mode* was not the first time it had been placed within the confines of a play. Tobias Smollett, in his comedy, *The Reprisal* in 1757, had the Irish lieutenant, O'Clabber, sing "Ye Swains of the Shannon, fair Sheelah is gone" to the tune of "Ellin a Roon." The song may first have been associated with the theatre in 1729 at the start of the ballad-opera craze, when Coffey directed that one of the songs in his *The Beggar's Wedding*, "How bashful Maids appear," be sung to the tune of "Ellen-a-Roon."[5]

Charles Macklin, the author of *Love a-la-Mode*, had provided texts for the songs in his farce with the facility for song writing that resulted from his youthful training as a strolling player. Macklin zealously kept his playscript from publishers and rival producers and threatened with prosecution anyone in London or the provinces who attempted to pirate his work.[6] Hence, it is interesting to note its frequent performances by the American Company between 1768 and 1774.

[24]

The Serenading Song

sung in

THE CONSTANT COUPLE, or A TRIP TO THE JUBILEE

A Comedy by George Farquhar

George Farquhar (1678–1707) | *Daniel Purcell (ca. 1660–1717)*

(He knocks)
swore; The Sign was So! She an - swer'd No!
tr
tr
tr
tr
(He knocks)
The Sign was So! She an - swer'd No! No,
p
(somewhat slower)
no, No, no! A - gain he
tr
mf
p
mp
sigh'd, a - gain he pray'd; No, Da - mon, no,

no, no, no, no! I am a - fraid. Con - si - der,
Da - - mon, I am a Maid; con - si - - der, Da - - mon,
no, no, no, no, no, no, no! I am a Maid.
(tempo I) mp
At last his Sighs and Tears made way; She rose and
mp

mf
soft - ly turn'd the Key. "Come in," she said, "but do not,
mf
do not stay! I may con - clude, you will be
f
f
f
rude, But if you are, you may. I may con -
p
p
f
f
clude you will be rude, But if you are, you may!
p
rit.
f
p
rit.
f

SIR HARRY WILDAIR, who "affects humourous gaiety and freedom in his behaviour," is on the other side of the door to Lady Lurewell's apartment when his "serenading song" is heard. The lady is "of a jilting temper, proceeding from a resentment of her wrongs from Men," and takes her revenge by plotting against her suitors. Her feelings are eventually assuaged by the discovery that the twelve-year absence of her lover, Colonel Standard, has been due to a misunderstanding.[1]

The comedy, first performed at Drury Lane in November 1699, brought together three men often associated at the theatre during the next decade. Daniel Purcell, who set the song, had made a solid contribution of music to the stage since his arrival in London in 1695, the year his famous brother Henry died, and was to furnish further settings for the author.[2] George Farquhar had come from Ireland a year or so before he wrote *The Constant Couple*, the second—and one of the most popular—of his plays. Robert Wilks, who played that "airy gentleman," Sir Harry, was the author's friend and fellow Irishman; he performed other leading roles in Farquhar's comedies in the course of a distinguished career.

The effective manner in which Purcell's music enhances the meaning of Farquhar's song shows why the composer was in such demand by contemporary dramatists. The closed door to Lady Lurewell's apartment provided the means for substituting another voice in the event that the actor in the role could not sing. Two other performers of the song besides Wilks are mentioned in the printed editions of the music, William Pate and John Freeman, both professional theatre singers.[3]

There were more than a score of performances of the comedy recorded on the colonial stage from the first in Norfolk, Virginia, in 1751 through 1774 in Charleston, South Carolina. The second known performance was also in Virginia; Williamsburg saw it, "with Entertainments of Singing and Dancing between the Acts," on April 17, 1752, shortly before the arrival of the Hallam Company, who had it in their repertoire. On that date Sir Harry Wildair was played by Thomas Kean, who in partnership with Walter Murray and others managed a troupe that was dwindling away.[4]

The Hallam Company's Sir Harry in 1753 was John Singleton. Lewis Hallam, Jr., succeeded him in the role for all performances of the play given by the American Company with one exception: Henrietta Osborne, appearing with the company in Charleston in 1766, played Sir Harry, a casting that followed the London fashion of assigning the role to women. When Mrs. Osborne joined the newly organized Virginia Company of Comedians in 1768 she appeared in Williamsburg as Sir Harry, dancing a minuet "in character" in the fifth act with Miss Yapp, who played Lady Lurewell's maid.[5]

[25]

Dear Pretty Youth

sung in

THE TEMPEST, or THE ENCHANTED ISLAND

Altered from the Play by William Shakespeare

Unidentified

Henry Purcell (1659–1695)

can you, can you sleep, how can you, can you sleep When I, when I__ am_ by? When
6 6
I, when I__ am_ by? Were__ I__ with you__ all__ Night__ to_ be, Me-
thinks I cou'd, me - thinks I cou'd, I cou'd from Sleep be__ free; Me -
thinks I cou'd, me - thinks I could from Sleep, I cou'd from Sleep be_ free.

Adagio
A - las, a - las, my Dear, you're cold, cold as
Adagio
a tempo
Stone. You must no long - er, no, no long - er, no, no long - er
6 6 6 6 6
no, no long-er, long-er be a - lone. But be with me, my
6 #
Dear, my Dear, Dear, Dear, but be with me, my
7 6 7 6 7 6 7 6

Dear, And I in each Arm, and I in each
Arm, will hug you, hug you close, Will hug you, hug you
close, hug you close and keep you warm, Will hug you, hug you
rit.
close, Will hug you, hug you close, hug you close and keep you warm.
rit.

WHEN Ariel, the airy spirit in *The Tempest*, reminded Prospero, his master, that "once thou call'd me up at midnight to fetch dew from the still vexed Bermoothes [Bermudas]," he provided Virginians with their first theatre-associated tradition.

It has been assumed that Shakespeare found the nucleus of his plot in a letter that William Strachey, secretary of the Virginia colony, wrote to a friend from Jamestown. In it Strachey, a survivor, described the storm and shipwreck of the *Sea Venture* in the Bermudas in July of 1609 en route from London to Virginia. Strachey had once owned a share in the Blackfriar's Theatre, which Shakespeare's company took over in 1608.[1]

Shakespeare furnished his play with songs and a masque, but by the eighteenth century both play and music had undergone the changes that made them into "something rich and strange." The seventeenth-century dramatist Sir William Davenant, who claimed to be Shakespeare's natural son, collaborated with John Dryden in 1667 in altering the plot and providing new music. Several years later their version was "made into an Opera by Mr. [Thomas] Shadwell, having all New in it: as Scenes, Machines, . . . all things was perform'd in it so Admirably well, that not any succeeding Opera got more Money."[2]

The Restoration version added Dorinda as sister to Miranda, who had never seen a mortal man except her father, Prospero. The addition of a male character, Hippolito, who had never seen a woman, was Davenant's suggestion. These characters remained in the play until the middle of the nineteenth century. The songs were equally long-lived. New music was composed to replace earlier settings, and entirely new songs, both text and music, were added to the older ones in the play.[3]

"Dear Pretty Youth" was among the songs that Henry Purcell furnished for a revival of the play in 1695, the last year of his life. He had been "very early in life solicited to compose for the stage," and had contributed music to some fifty theatre productions, several of them musically embellished enough to be considered operas.[4]

"Dear Pretty Youth" was printed in song collections for the next twenty-five years, and was billed with Dorinda's part for at least twice that many. Neither it nor another song that was set for Dorinda by James Hart in the 1674 version was printed in the play. Their interpolation probably occurred in the scene (scene 3, Act IV of the Dryden-Davenant adaptation) in which Ferdinand thinks he has mortally wounded Hippolito in a duel. Prospero, entering with Dorinda, tells her to look yonder: "Alas, poor Girl, thou hast no Man." Dorinda, ignorant of death, replies, "He lies asleep, Sir, shall I waken him?" and kneels by Hippolito's side to try to rouse him. It is at this point that she must have sung "Dear Pretty Youth."[5]

By 1770, the American Company was musically capable of producing "*The Tempest, or the Inchanted Island*, written by Shakespeare, alter'd by Dryden," with all the "Scenes and Machines" and the "Grand Masque of *Neptune and Amphitrite*."[6] The first colonial performances were described as among the "greatest attempts ever made by the Performers in this part of the World" with "good Taste shown in the disposition of the Machinery and Decorations." That the audiences thoroughly approved of what was termed "one of the most pleasing Pieces" to make its appearance in the American theatre is shown by the sixteen performances recorded in the next four years and by the fact that it was one of the first plays to be revived following the Revolution.[7]

The Tempest probably was performed for the first time in Williamsburg during the 1770–71 season, when the company was appearing there and at Annapolis, where the play was given sometime before November 7, 1771, with Nancy Hallam playing the role of Dorinda.[8]

{26}

Wher' Did You Borrow That Last Sigh?

sung in

THE LOST LADY

A Play by Sir William Berkeley

Sir William Berkeley (1609–1677)

William Lawes (1602–1645)

THIS song was written for a play that never appeared on the colonial stage, but because of the author's association with Virginia it is included here. Sir William Berkeley wrote *The Lost Lady* for a performance at the court of Charles I in 1637, five years before he was appointed governor of Virginia.

The music for the song, preserved in a manuscript in the composer's hand, was the work of Berkeley's fellow courtier William Lawes, one of the king's favorite musicians. Lawes and his more famous elder brother, Henry, were among the accomplished musicians from whom it was customary for court poets such as Suckling and Herrick to solicit musical settings to enhance their verse.[1]

Eight years after *The Lost Lady* was acted "with much applause" before the Court and at Blackfriar's Theatre, the English Civil War separated both author and composer from the scenes of their collaboration. In June 1645 Governor Berkeley, after a futile trip to England to obtain aid for the colonies against the Indians, returned to Virginia to remain there until after the Restoration. The following September William Lawes, serving in the king's forces besieged at Chester, "betray'd," it was said, "by his own adventurousness," was "casually shot" while the king watched the Royalist rout from the city's wall.[2]

The title of Berkeley's play in which Lawes's music was heard refers to its heroine, Milesia, who is the lost lady. She has escaped the death planned for her by her treacherous uncle and, disguised as Acanthe, the Moor, with a gift for divination, arrives on the scene just as her sorrowing betrothed, Lord Lysicles, is about to marry an equally reluctant Hermione at the insistence of the latter's father. On the eve of the wedding Hermione gives an order to Phillida, her lady in waiting: "Philly, take thy lute and sing the song was given thee last." Whereupon Phillida exits, the song is heard off stage, and "the song being ended, re-enter Phillida." This awkward procedure may indicate one of the occasions when a song had to be performed off stage by a professional member of the theatre band, whose lute players were also vocalists. Generally, the actors in this period were expected to be competent musicians who could sing and accompany themselves on the lute.[3]

The play was licensed for printing in 1638. Over a hundred years later Robert Dodsley reprinted it in his *Select Collection of Old Plays* (1744). During the Commonwealth, it was given privately at Knowlton by the household and guests of Sir Thomas Peyton. It was revived on the Restoration stage in 1661, when Samuel Pepys saw it twice, deciding he was more pleased with it the second time than he had been on the first occasion. Berkeley, reinstated as governor, was summoned to England to appear before the Council for Foreign Plantations, but arrived too late to witness these performances.[4]

[27]

There's Not a Swain

sung in

DAMON AND PHILLIDA

A Ballad Opera by Colley Cibber

Anthony Henley (d. 1711) *Henry Purcell (1659–1695)*

But you ap - pear so se - vere, that trem - - bling with Fear,
My Heart goes pit - a - pat, pit - a - pat all the while.
When I cry, "Must I dye?" you make no re - ply,
But look shy, And with a scorn - ful Eye, kill me, kill me

CORYDON, the old shepherd, has urged the rustic Cymon and his brother Mopsus to compete for the hand of Corydon's daughter Phillida—who loves the inconstant Damon. Cymon sings his stuttering suit in this song, the opening number of Cibber's little pastoral farce set in "the Arcadian Fields."[1]

"There's not a Swain" was taken from the theatre songs of "the late famous Mr. Henry Purcell," whose music was the source of tunes for many of the ballad operas of the period, beginning with *The Beggar's Opera* in 1728, a third of a century after the composer's death. Purcell had composed it originally as a hornpipe for the "First Musick" (part of the instrumental preludes) to his opera *The Fairy Queen* in 1692. Late in 1693 Purcell participated in revising the music as a song setting for "There's not a Swain" in a revival of Fletcher's *Rule a Wife*. The song with text by Anthony Henley was printed in *The Gentleman's Journal* for April 1694. Thirty-five years later the text and tune were adapted for Cymon's song.[2]

Henry Carey, who had composed two songs for Cibber's *The Provok'd Husband* the previous year, adapted the tunes, including one of his own, to the words of the other fourteen songs in *Damon and Phillida*. Cibber had fashioned his "new, diverting Pastoral" from the subplot salvaged after the failure of his *Love in a Riddle*. He presented it anonymously on August 16, 1729, a little more than six months after his original play had been hissed off the stage.[3]

Damon and Phillida was "among the best Plays, Operas, Farces, and Pantomimes exhibited in any of the London Theatres these ten Years past" which the Hallam Company brought to Virginia in 1752. It was so popular on the colonial stage that more than three dozen performances are recorded, including two in Williamsburg, from the Murray-Kean period of 1750 through 1774.[4]

In a Hallam Company cast for a New York performance on September 17, 1753, the stuttering Cymon was played by Miller, an actor whose name, either by kinship or coincidence was the same as that of the original Cymon at Drury Lane.[5] The playbills that survive for the following seasons show Cymon in the American Company's performances as played at first by Tomlinson and then by Adam Hallam, younger brother of Lewis, Jr. After 1767 the part was taken by Thomas Wall, frequently cast in comic and singing roles. Cymon was played by Parker in the Virginia Company cast for the Williamsburg performance of 1768. Probably Wall was Cymon when Williamsburg saw the last performance of the play recorded there, in 1771.[6]

[28]

When Damon Languish'd

sung in

THE GAMESTER

A Tragedy by Edward Moore

Edward Moore (1712–1757) *James Oswald (d. 1769)*

Mo - ments of De - light, how sweet! But Ah! how swift they
flew. The sun - ny Hill, The flow - - - 'ry Vale, The
Gar - den and the Grove Have e - cho'd to his
ar - dent Tale, And Vows of end - less Love.

2

The Conquest gain'd, he left his Prize,
He left her to complain,
To tell of Joy with weeping Eyes,
And measure Time by Pain.
But Heav'n will take the Lover's Part
In Pity to despair,
And the last Sigh that rends the Heart
Shall waft the Spirit there.

THANK Heaven my Griefs are none of these," exclaims the melancholy Mrs. Beverley, after she has thanked Lucy, her maid, for soothing her with this song. Her affliction is not the loss of her husband's love, but his feverish addiction to the gaming tables, which has been stimulated by the treacherous Stukely.

"The Passions are exquisitely touched," stated a newspaper puff for a March 4, 1766, performance in Charleston, South Carolina, describing the play for those who had not seen it the preceding year. "The Scenes are in Domestick Life . . . the Catastrophe severely just." The moral is summed up "in the Words of the Author . . . Want of Prudence is Want of Virtue."[1]

The Gamester became part of the Hallam Company's repertoire on February 4, 1754, only a year after its first performance at Drury Lane. Through the next two decades the play was given repeatedly everywhere on the colonial circuit. The short-lived splinter company that played Virginia and Maryland in 1768–69 gave it on May 20, 1768 in Williamsburg.[2]

Edward Moore, who wrote this "Domestick" tragedy, was an author, poet, and editor of a satirical periodical, *The World*. Garrick, who had produced other plays of Moore's at Drury Lane, doctored the plot or, as he put it, "thickened the pudding a little" to suit the taste of the audience. The result gained ready acceptance, as the speed of its appearance on the provincial boards shows: it was given at Bath within a month.[3]

Mrs. Clarkson took the part of Lucy, the maid with "the sympathizing heart," in New York in 1754. Others who performed the role over the years were Nancy Hallam in the Charleston performance of March 1766, Miss Wainwright in Philadelphia in 1767, where she was billed as "Lucy, with a Song," and Miss Richardson in New York in 1773.[4]

James Oswald, a composer and cellist whose music aroused the emotions of his audiences, set Moore's song text. When he had left his native Scotland for London, the *Scots Magazine* for October 1741, published an anonymous "Poetical Epistle" lamenting his departure. The poem referred to the "encircling Fair" hanging attentive on each vibration of his "trembling String," his melting notes, and the delight in his gay tunes. In a letter of 1765 Benjamin Franklin mentioned the tears brought to the eyes of Oswald's listeners by his playing on the violoncello.[5]

[29]

If the Swain We Sigh For

sung in

MIDAS

A Burletta by Kane O'Hara

Kane O'Hara (1711–1782) *Unidentified*

f
'tis to please. If the Fright we loath ad -
mf
dress us, How de - - light - ful 'tis to teize!
mp
p
f
If the Fright we loath ad - dress us, how
mf
de - - light - - - - - - - - ful 'tis to teize.
tr
mp

MIDAS, first given in Dublin in January 1762, was performed for the first time in London at Covent Garden Theatre on February 22, 1764. Five years later the American Company added it to the stock pieces in their repertoire. And in 1771, two years after its first appearance on the colonial stage, the music for *Midas*, set "for Harpsichord, Voice, German Flute, Violin, or Guitar," was advertised for sale at the Printing Office in Williamsburg.[1]

A parody of Italian *opera seria*, *Midas* involves the Olympian gods with mortals. Apollo, on Mt. Olympus, incenses his father Jove by his saucy interference in Jove's quarrel with Juno. Dashed to earth by a thunderbolt hurled by his irate father, Apollo appropriates the guitar and "greasy old tatters" of a shepherd frightened away by his spectacular arrival. Thus disguised he charms all the girls and causes a quarrel between Sileno's daughters Nysa and Daphne. Nysa is "jealous of his taste and bad eye" in preferring Daphne. Nysa's attitude toward the unwelcome attentions of her own elderly suitor, Midas, is revealed in this song.[2]

In the first performance of *Midas* at Covent Garden (and for many years thereafter) Nysa was played by Isabella Hallam, sister of Lewis Hallam, Jr., of the American Company, and Apollo by George Mattocks, the actor-singer whom she married during the Easter holidays the following year.[3] In colonial performances of *Midas* from 1769 until 1774, Nysa was played by another daughter of the theatre, the young singing actress Maria Storer.

Evidently the music in *Midas* was popular in Virginia. Nysa's song, under the title "A Song in Midas," was one of a number of theatre songs that Robert Bolling and his son copied into their manuscript music books at Chellowe plantation. At Thomas Jefferson's Monticello a different "Song from Midas," without words and set for harpsichord, was in a manuscript book belonging to Mrs. Jefferson.[4]

[30]

All around the Maypole

sung in

MIDAS

A Burletta by Kane O'Hara

Kane O'Hara (1711–1782) *Unidentified*

mf
and what not. All a-round the May-pole how they trot, Hot, pot,
mp
and brown Ale they've got.
There is old Si-len-o
mf
mp
frisks like a mad Lad, glad to see us so sad, Cap'r-ing, vap'r-ing,
while Pol scrap-ing coax-es the Las-ses as he did the Dad. All a-round the May-pole

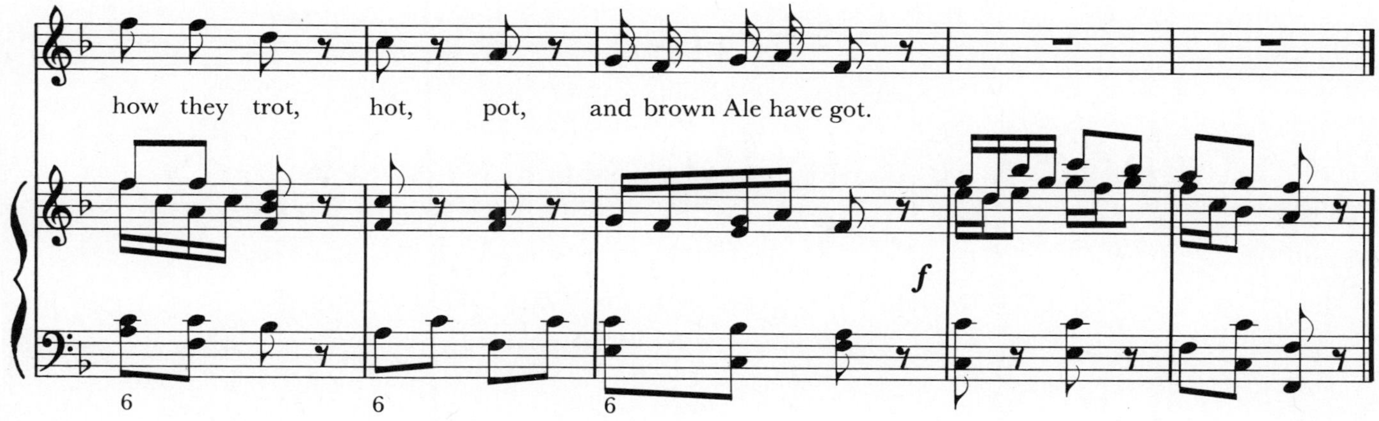

KANE O'HARA, the Irish author of several popular burlettas, of which *Midas* was the first, was considered to have "exquisite taste in music" and to be "very happy in producing rhymes and adapting new words to old music." According to John O'Keefe, the Irish dramatist, O'Hara wrote *Midas* at the urging of Lord Mornington, an accomplished amateur musician and father of the Duke of Wellington. Mornington led the band (i.e., the orchestra) at concerts in the Great Room in Fishamble Street, Dublin, where the Right Honorable William Brownlow played the harpsichord. Brownlow is said to have helped select and arrange the music for *Midas*.[1]

O'Hara's burletta was a burlesque of the ancient tale of Midas, the semi-legendary king of Phrygia, to whom the resentful Apollo gave the ears of an ass because Midas declared Pan superior to Apollo as a flute player. Part of O'Hara's fun was in exchanging Pan's classic pipes for the bagpipes (the "chanter") and in having Pol, the disguised Apollo, "god of Music and King of Parnass" [Parnassus] "clatter the guittar with tinkling divine."[2]

When Damaetas, the spurned suitor of Daphne, wants Pan's help in removing his rival Pol, he twits Pan with the girls' desertion of him and his "chanter" for the brighter charms of Pol and his guitar, and jeers Pan in this song.[3]

The burletta and John Fawcett as Damaetus both made their first appearance at Covent Garden on the same night. Fawcett was an apprentice pupil of Dr. Arne's who had hired him out to Drury Lane two years earlier.

Thomas Wall, the tenor singer and actor, was the American Company's Damaetas, and was undoubtedly heard in the role in Williamsburg.[4]

[31]

While Gentle Parthenisa Walks

sung in

THE TENDER HUSBAND, or THE ACCOMPLISH'D FOOLS

A Comedy by Sir Richard Steele

Sir Richard Steele (1672–1729) — *Daniel Purcell (ca. 1660–1717)*

While gen -
- - tle Par - the - ni - sa walks, And sweet - - - - ly smiles,
And sweet - - - - ly smiles and gai - - - - ly talks,
p
A thou - sand Shafts a - round her fly, A thou - sand

Swains un - heed - ed die; A thou - sand Shafts a round her
fly, A thou - sand Swains, a thou - sand Swains un - heed - ed die.
D.C. ending Fine.
D.C. ending Fine.
(a little faster)
die. If then she la - bors to be seen, With all her kill - ing
Air and Mien, From so much Beau - ty, So much Art, what Mor - tal can se -

STEELE dedicated *The Tender Husband*, his third play, to Joseph Addison, to whom he attributed "many applauded strokes in it." Both writers later were associated with the *Tatler*, the *Spectator*, and the *Guardian*, periodicals much valued in the colonies.[1]

This comedy with its songs could have been among the unidentified plays given at Williamsburg's first theatre some dozen or so years after the first London performance. The play was given in Williamsburg on April 22, 1771 by the American Company, with *The Honest Yorkshireman* as the afterpiece.[2]

In Steele's plot the resourceful Captain Clerimont, disguised as an artist, courts Biddy under her aunt's nose while he pretends to paint her picture. Clerimont entertains the ladies with a fictitious tale of a fellow portrait painter who, having fallen in love and eloped with his subject, "turned Poet" and wrote a sonnet about her. When Clerimont declares he knows the words by heart, Biddy wants to hear them and he complies. Her cousin Humphrey suggests that if the sonnet were sung "it would make a pretty Catch." The captain then sends for his servant, "who has a voice." The play text directs: "Here it is sung."

Other plays had songs that were read or recited before

they were sung, possibly because the author wanted his verses heard without distraction, or perhaps to fix them in the minds of the audience as a way to popularize the song.[3]

Of fourteen incidental songs that Steele wrote and had set for his plays, there were two others in *The Tender Husband*: "Why, Belvidera," also set by Daniel Purcell, and the song in the comical scene of the music lesson—in which Lewis Ramondon, the composer, played himself as the "spinet-master."[4]

Purcell's setting of "Gentle Parthenisa" was printed in *The Monthly Mask of Vocal Music* in 1705, the same year the play was produced. Steele's song was reset at least twice. It was published in 1741 with a group of Arne's early theatre songs, and was both set and sung by Daniel Sullivan, an alto who sang in Handel's oratorios.[5]

In the Philadelphia cast of March 1770, Captain Clerimont was played by Byerley, who may have sung the song himself instead of calling in a servant. He probably played the part in Williamsburg in 1771, when he appeared there in one of the singing roles in *Love in a Village*. Byerley had singing roles in other plays while with the American Company from 1769 to 1773, but was no longer with the company in its final season in Charleston. It has been surmised that he may have been the Thomas Byerley who, in February 1774, announced plans to open a school in New York which would stress the use of English speech.[6]

[32]

The Modern Beau

sung in

THE HONEST YORKSHIREMAN

A Ballad Opera by Henry Carey

Henry Carey (ca. 1687–1743) | *Henry Carey*

Taste in at - tire, The Ladies shall lan - guish for thee!
Such flaunt-ing, gal - lant - ing and jaunt - ing and fro - lick - ing thou shall
see!
Thou ne'er like a Clown shalt quit Lon - don, sweet Town,
To live in thy own Coun - try.

2

A skimming dish Hat provide
  With little more Brim than Lace,
Nine Hairs on a side
To a Pigtail ty'd
  Will set off thy jolly broad Face.
Such flaunting, etc. . . .

3

Go get thee a Footman's Frock
  And a Cudgel quite up to your Nose;
Then Frizz like a Shock
And plaister thy Block
  And buckle thy Shoes at thy Toes.
Such flaunting, etc. . . .

4

A Brace of Ladies fair
  To pleasure thee shall strive;
In a Chaise and a Pair
They shall take the Air
  And thou on the Box shall drive.
Such flaunting, etc. . . .

5

Convert thy Acres to Cash
  And saw the Timber down;
Who'd keep such Trash
And not cut a Flash
  Or enjoy the Delights of the Town?
Such flaunting, etc. . . .

T*HE Honest Yorkshireman* was one of the most popular ballad-opera afterpieces on the colonial stage, with nearly two dozen performances on record between the advent of the Hallam Company in 1752 and its final season of 1774. It is unlikely, then, that a Williamsburg audience heard this song for the first time when William Verling as Gaylove sang it at a performance given by the newly organized Virginia Company on April 4, 1768.[1]

Verling was one of several colonial performers to appear in the role of the audacious young barrister Gaylove in Carey's afterpiece.

His song of sartorial advice is addressed to Samuel Sapscull, Junior, the oafish country squire who has come to London to marry Arabella at the behest of her uncle, Sir Penurious Muckworm. Gaylove, in love with Arabella, pretends to be the uncle and waylays the Yorkshire squire when he arrives. By telling him that Arabella "loves everything to the tip top of the Mode," Gaylove persuades Sapscull to buy new clothes; he himself dons the old. Thus attired, Gaylove hoodwinks the uncle into believing him the Yorkshire suitor and so wins the bride. The Yorkshire-born Carey's choice of title for his ballad opera, *The Honest Yorkshireman*, would have been understood by his contemporaries as an allusion to the proverbial cunning and trickery attributed to Yorkshire natives.

Gaylove's "Come hither" song was among Carey's most popular airs. Nearly thirty years after its first performance its tune reappeared in a dialogue and duet, "If a Rival thy Character Draw," in Kane O'Hara's burletta, *Midas*, where it would have been heard again on the colonial stage.

Henry Carey wrote *The Honest Yorkshireman* as well as composed the music for eight of its twenty songs. His ability to combine poetry and music was praised by Dr. Charles Burney, who, as a young apprentice to Thomas Arne, then composer to Drury Lane, had written the accompaniments to some of Carey's tunes. Burney regarded "Honest Harry Carey" and Rousseau as the "only bards in modern times" who achieved this combination, citing *The Honest Yorkshireman* and the *Devin du Village* as examples.[2]

Sir John Hawkins, Burney's rival as a music historian, acknowledged the inventiveness of Carey's airs, but complained that Carey was so little skilled in music that he was "just able to set a bass." Nevertheless, Carey had studied with such musicians as Geminiani and Roseingrave, as well as the unidentified Olaus Westeinson Linnert.[3]

The actor-singer William Quelch probably played the part of Gaylove in Williamsburg during the season of 1761–62 as he had in the preceding New York season. When *The Honest Yorkshireman* was given in Williamsburg ten years later on April 22, 1771, Stephen Woolls undoubtedly had the role—as he did in Philadelphia the following year. His Arabella then, and probably in Williamsburg, was Maria Storer, in the role her mother had performed in England a quarter of a century before.[4]

[33]

My Passion in Vain

sung in

THE MAID OF THE MILL

A Comic Opera by Isaac Bickerstaffe

Isaac Bickerstaffe (ca. 1735–1812) — *Giacchino Cocchi (ca. 1715–ca. 1804)*

makes it ap - pear. En - rap - tur'd I gaze, when I
touch her I trem-ble, when I touch her I trem - ble. And
speak_ to, And hear_ her And speak_ to,
and hear_ her with fault' - ring_ and
f
p

Fear, With fault' - - ring and Fear,
With fault' - - ring and Fear
mf
By how many cru - el I - de - as tor - men - ted, I -
p
de - as tor - men - ted, My Mind's in a fer - ment, it

free - zes and burns, my Mind's in a fer - ment, it free - zes and
burns. This mo - ment I wish what the next is re -
pen - ted, the next is re - pen - ted. This mo - ment
I wish what the next is re - pen - ted,

what the next is re - pen - ted, is re - pen - ted,
while Love, Rage, and Jea - lou - sy rack
me by turns; Love, Rage, and Jea - lou - sy rack me by turns. This
mo - ment I wish what the next is re - pen - ted, the next is re - pen - ted;
p

While Love, Rage, and Jea - lou - sy___ rack__ me by turns, while
Love,_ Rage, and Jea - lou - sy___ rack__ me by turns. Rack,
rack, rack me by turns. Rack, rack, rack me by
turns by turns, rack me, rack__ me by turns, by

LORD AIMWORTH "can't read, can't think, can't do anything" because he is in love with Patty, the miller's daughter, who is betrothed to Farmer Giles. He tries to dissuade her from the marriage. But Patty, who believes she must keep to her lower station in life, allows him to think she loves Giles. After she leaves, Aimworth pours forth his feelings in this song as he paces the marble portico of his country estate.

Samuel Arnold, the twenty-four-year-old composer to Covent Garden, selected and arranged the music for Isaac Bickerstaffe's comic opera. He contributed four of the thirty-seven songs himself and compiled the rest (and the overture) from the music of nineteen other composers. This song he set to an air by Giacchino Cocchi, an Italian musician residing in London, who later directed the fashionable concerts in Soho that the Virginian, Arthur Lee of Stratford Hall, attended.[1]

The music of the opera proved popular, and to keep it from being appropriated, Covent Garden held it in manuscript for some months after the first performance. When Robert Bremner published the London, 1765, edition for "Voice, Harpsichord or Violin," it contained the warning "that whoever Presumes to Print or write out for Sale any Song in this Opera, will be prosecuted by the Author and the Proprietors with the utmost rigour of the Law." By 1771, however, the music was widely available. The *Virginia Gazette* advertised it for "Harpsichord, Violin, German Flute, and Hautboy," among the music that had just arrived "by the *Virginia*, Captain Robinson."[2]

Isaac Bickerstaffe, an Irish-born dramatist and former officer of the marines, based his comic opera on Samuel Richardson's popular novel *Pamela*. It was one of the five musical plays by Bickerstaffe in the colonial repertoire. It probably was performed in Williamsburg sometime during the season in which the music was advertised for sale.[3]

The Maid of the Mill made its first American appearance in New York in May 1769, the same month that the author's play, *The Padlock*, with music by Dibdin, was added to the repertoire. The following month *The Maid of the Mill* was among the plays listed as "read" and "the Songs sung" at the Assembly Room in Philadelphia. In July, at a concert in New York's Vauxhall Garden, Stephen Woolls, Lewis Hallam, Jr., and Nancy Hallam sang selections from both *The Maid of the Mill* and *The Padlock*.[4]

Lewis Hallam played Lord Aimworth with the American Company, the role which his brother-in-law, George Mattocks, had created in London.

[34]

Solemn Dirge

sung in

ROMEO AND JULIET

A Tragedy by William Shakespeare

Unidentified

Thomas A. Arne (1710–1778)

At the beginning of the Procession the Trumpets advance with the Drums and sound the following Solemn Notes between which the Bell tolls, till they are off the Stage.

Solemn Dirge

Trebles
mf
Ah, hap - less Maid
Tenor
mf
Bass
Ah, hap - less
tr
mf
tr
Doom'd to the gap-ing Jaws of a cold, cold com - fort-less and drear - y Tomb.
Maid Doom'd to the gap-ing Jaws of a com - fort-less and drear - y Tomb.
f
Thy Mar - riage Song is chang'd to mourn-ful Dirge, Thy
f
f

(rit.)
brid-al, brid-al bed to a black Fun' - ral Hearse.
brid - al
Very slow and solemn.
tr
(rit.)
Fl., strings mf
Go on immediately
[Bell]
f
Hark,
pp
mf
f
(Bass)
mf
hark, how with aw - ful Pause The So - - lemn
p
mf

Bell
In Death like Sounds
Tolls her un-time-ly
Tolls
Knell, her un-time-ly Knell;
In Death-like Sounds tolls her un-
Tolls
Tolls
(f)
Adagio
(rit.)
(Fine)
(Solo, two trebles)
time-ly Knell.
(p) She was her Pa-rent's Sole De-
(Solo, tenor)
Adagio
(Fine)
(rit.)
pp (strings)

light, They had but one, one on - ly child.
Tutti
mf She was her Pa - rent's Sole De - light, They had but
mf
one, one on - ly child. (p) Since Death has torn her
2 Soli
(Solo bass)
(p)

Repeat the foregoing movement, viz., Hark, hark, till all the Procession is over.

THE "Solemn Dirge," first introduced as part of Juliet's funeral procession in *Romeo and Juliet* at Covent Garden in 1750, and in the colonies in 1759, probably was first performed in Williamsburg in the season of 1761–62. Several performances had been given at Annapolis, followed by another in Upper Marlborough, on the company's route to the Virginia capital. The last Annapolis performance was billed with the familiar "Funeral Procession and a Solemn Dirge as perform'd at the Theatre Royal in Covent Garden."[1]

The addition of Arne's "Dirge" had helped Covent Garden score an initial success over Drury Lane on the opening night of the two theatres' rival performances of Shakespeare's tragedy. Four days later music by William Boyce to a text by Garrick was added to the funeral procession at Drury Lane. Boyce and Arne, one the son of a cabinetmaker and the other of an upholsterer, were the foremost native English composers of the eighteenth century. They "were frequently concurrents at the theatres and in each other's way," according to Charles Burney.[2]

The play, with its much admired additional scene and music, continued to be performed frequently at both theatres for many seasons. The interpolation of the dirge was so popular with London audiences that the text used at Drury Lane and that used at Covent Garden were reset by other composers.[3]

The way in which the American playbills featured the dirge and the vocal performers in the funeral procession demonstrates how closely the colonial theatre followed the music pattern of the London stage.[4]

There is no way of knowing if the music was sung just as Arne had written it, since parts were shifted to accommodate the voices that were available and to meet existing conditions. It is quite evident, however, that the colonial company never found itself in the straits to which an English company of hand-to-mouth strollers was reduced when Romeo had to toll his own knell and Juliet sing her own dirge.[5]

At a New York performance in 1773, when Nancy Hallam, who played Juliet, sang "The Soldier Tir'd" from Arne's *Artaxerxes* between the acts, she was accompanied by the band of His Majesty's Twenty-third Regiment. It would seem probable that the band also provided the full accompaniment called for in the score of the "Solemn Dirge." Arne's instrumental score included, besides flutes and strings, a bell for the funeral tolling, trumpets, and muffled kettledrums.[6]

The "Solemn Dirge" undoubtedly was heard again in a performance of *Romeo and Juliet* in Williamsburg during the 1762–63 season of unidentified plays. One of the vocal parts would have been taken by William Quelch, who had sung in a New York performance of the play the preceding spring. On December 21, 1762, Quelch was initiated into the Williamsburg Masonic Lodge, which, probably like other lodges in the colonies and in England, frequently patronized the theatre.[7]

[35]

Let's Sing of Stage Coaches

sung in

THE STAGE COACH

A Comedy by George Farquhar

George Farquhar (1678–1707) | *John Eccles (1668–1735)*

whist-ling and flog - ging, The Coach-man drives on, With a "Hay, gee - up!
Geeup! hay ho!" With a hay, gee, Dob - bin, hay ho! hay!
gee - up, gee - up, gee - up, hay ho! Gee - up, gee - up,
gee - up, hay ho!" With a "Hay, gee, Dob - bin, hay ho!"

2

In Coaches thus strowling
Who wou'd not be rowling
With Nymphs on each side?
Still prattling and playing
Our knees interplaying
We merrily ride
With a hay, etc.

3

Here Chance kindly mixes
All sorts and all Sexes,
More Females than Men;
We squeeze 'em, we ease 'em
The jolting does please 'em,
Drive jollyly then
With a hay, etc.

4

The harder you're driving
The more 'tis reviving,
Nor fear we to fall;
For if the Coach tumble,
We'll all have a rare jumble
And then uptails all
With a hay, etc.

THE uncertainties of travel in that "tedious, tiresome, dull, jolting vehicle" of eighteenth-century transportation supplied the motivation for Farquhar's farce, *The Stage Coach.*[1] An odd assortment of characters are stranded at an inn by the whims and greed of the coachman and the landlord. Among them are Isabella, her avaricious old uncle, and the slow-witted Nicodemus Somebody, a self-satisfied country squire whom the uncle intends Isabella to marry.

The passengers, expected to share equally the difficulties and the expense, quibble over the division of the bill for their inadequate dinners. Nicodemus demands that Isabella pay a crown for her share, although she has had nothing but hartshorn drops, the infallible remedy of eighteenth-century ladies in distress. Then he tells her "and that you may not think you're hardly dealt by, I'll sing you the song that makes it Stage Coach Law."

The song was among the fifty or more that John Eccles, the composer, violinist, and "Master of the King's Band of Musick," set for the theatre between 1690 and the second decade of the eighteenth century. It demonstrates the vigor and roguish charm said to have characterized his compositions.[2]

The competent and comical Thomas Doggett, once described as "wearing a Farce in his Face," originated the part of Nicodemus. The only colonial actor identified as Nicodemus was Miller, who appeared with the Hallam Company during its first New York season in 1753–54. In another coincidence of casting, like that in the role of Cymon in *Damon and Phillida*, the English actor Miller had also played the role of Nicodemus.[3]

The Stage Coach was the sixth of the eight plays that George Farquhar, "whose Genius inclined very much to Comedy," contributed to the stage between 1698 and his death in 1707. In writing it he was said to have had the help of Peter Anthony Motteux, dramatist and editor of the *Gentleman's Journal*, the first of the monthly miscellanies (1691–94).[4]

Colonial playbills, library inventories, and book advertisements attest the popularity of Farquhar's plays in America. All eight were on the colonial stage at some time or other, several repeatedly, from 1736 to 1774. Performances of this farce were recorded from 1750 through the next decade by the Murray-Kean troupe, by the Hallams, and by the American Company, who probably played it in Williamsburg during their first tour of Virginia and Maryland in 1760–61.[5]

Four years after the first publication of Farquhar's *Collected Works* in 1714, the inventory of Councilor Edmund Berkeley of Barn Elms, Middlesex County, Virginia, listed his "Collected Writings." Towards the end of the century, Farquhar's works were also listed in the 1782 inventory of the estate of George Washington's stepson, John Parke Custis, of Fairfax County.[6]

{36}

Cupid, God of Soft Persuasion

sung in

LOVE IN A VILLAGE

A Comic Opera by Isaac Bickerstaffe

Isaac Bickerstaffe (ca. 1735–1812) | *Felice de Giardini* (1716–1796)

part, Oh, seize some kind Oc-ca--sion, to re-ward a faith-ful
Heart; Seize, oh seize some kind Oc--ca--sion to re--ward a faith-ful
Heart.
pp
[Fine]
mf
Just--ly those we Ty--rants call, who the Bo--dy wou'd en-
[Fine]
mp

poco rit.
tr
thrall; Ty - - rants of more cru - el kind,__ Those who wou'd en - - slave the
tr
poco rit.
6 4 5 3
6 4 5 3
6
6 4 5 3♯
p a tempo
Mind. Cu - - pid, God of__ soft per - sua - - sion, Take a help - less__ Lo - - ver's
p
6
6 5
6
6
part,__ Oh,____ seize some kind Oc - ca - - sion, to re - ward a__ faith - ful
6
6 5
6
6
6 4 5 3
Heart;__ Seize, oh,__ seize__ some kind__ Oc - - ca - sion to__ re -

tr
ward a faith - ful Heart.
p
6
4
5
3
mf
What is gran - - deur? Foe to rest, Child - ish
mp
6
mum - - mer - y at best; Hap - - py I in hum - ble state; Catch, ye
3
5
6
poco rit, ad lib
Dal Signo al Fine
a tempo
Fools, at glitt - 'ring bait, Catch the bait. Cu - pid
(colla voce)

WHAT must have been the first book of theatre songs associated with Williamsburg was named for Maria Storer, the youngest of the singing actresses in the American Company. As Lucinda in *Love in a Village* she sang this song at a performance there on May 1, 1771. Before she arrived for the summer season, she already had received a tribute in the *Maryland Gazette* to her "fine genius." Poetical eulogies in the same newspaper in future seasons would mention her "powers of song, and musick's magic charm."[1]

The most significant tribute paid her, however, appeared in Williamsburg the year after her performance in *Love in a Village*, when William Rind's *Virginia Gazette* advertised: "Just publish'd . . . *The Storer, or The American Syren* . . . a Collection of the newest and most approv'd Songs." Its prototype, *The Brent, or the English Syren*, had been published in London in 1765 and was imported for sale in Virginia in 1768 among other songbooks "just arrived in the *Brilliant*."[2] *The Brent* was a songbook without music whose title complimented Charlotte Brent, the popular actress and favorite pupil of Dr. Arne. Its contents included contemporary theatre songs, such as "Young am I and sore afraid," sung by Miss Brent as the original Rosetta in *Love in a Village*.[3]

Although *The Storer* was advertised for several years, no copy has been found. Presumably it contained many of the same songs as *The Brent* but with American performers named, or, as in *The American Mock Bird*, published in New York in 1760, similar theatre songs but with the English singers still designated.[4]

The vocal talents of Maria Storer, undoubtedly nurtured by her mother, had been featured from the beginning of her theatre appearances.[5] As Lucinda, she played the part of one of the young people in *Love in a Village* whose romantic difficulties are caused by the interference of their elders. Her emotional state is reflected in her song. Compelled to meet her suitor in secret, she eventually succeeds in presenting him to her family as an itinerant "Musick Master," an introduction that further complicates the plot.

Thomas Arne, then composer to Covent Garden, furnished the music for nineteen of the forty-three songs in *Love in a Village*, six of them newly composed. Lucinda's song was set to an air by Felice de Giardini, one of the other fourteen composers whose works were selected for the opera. An Italian composer and violinist, his "great hand, taste, and style of playing," according to the music historian Charles Burney, "were universally admired." Cuthbert Ogle, who came to Williamsburg in 1755 and died before realizing his intention of teaching gentlemen to play in concert, had been associated with Giardini in a series of London concerts in 1751–52 and had brought with him to Virginia six of Giardini's sonatas among a large quantity of music.[6]

[37]

My Dolly Was the Fairest Thing

sung in

LOVE IN A VILLAGE

A Comic Opera by Isaac Bickerstaffe

Isaac Bickerstaffe (ca. 1735–1812) *George Frederic Handel (1685–1759)*

mf
And if for Sum - mer you wou'd seek, 'Twas paint - ed in her Eye, her
mp
Cheek; And if for Sum - mer you wou'd seek, 'Twas paint - ed in her Eye, her
Cheek.
mp
Her swell - ing Bos - om, tempt - ing
f
p
ripe, of fruit - ful Au - tumn was the Type; But when my ten - der Tale was
p
p

ROSETTA has run away from home to avoid meeting the man her family has chosen to be her husband. With the connivance of her school friend, Lucinda, she poses as a servant in Lucinda's home. There she falls in love with the gardener, who eventually is disclosed as the intended and heretofore reluctant suitor. One of the results of her deception is this song.

Squire Hawthorne, an old friend and neighbor, comes on the scene just as the supposed maid has mockingly repulsed the advances of Justice Woodcock, Lucinda's father, and has made her laughing exit. The squire soothes the ruffled Woodcock, who "has been a Wag in his time," and recalls his own youth in this song.

The air was an adaptation of Handel's "Let me wander not unseen" from his *L'Allegro, il Penseroso, ed il Moderato*, based on the poems of John Milton.[1] Handel's music had been appropriated for songs in ballad plays and farces beginning with *The Beggar's Opera*, whose airs he is said to have told Pepusch he greatly admired.[2]

John Beard played Squire Hawthorne in the original London production; Stephen Woolls had the squire's role in the colonies. A letter from "A Gentleman Contributor" to a Philadelphia newspaper on January 22, 1767, both criticizing and complimenting the players, described Woolls as "almost equal to Beard in Hawthorne." Woolls was one of the "eminent performers . . . in the Singing Way" whom the American Company had recruited by 1766 in order to present English comic opera, of which *Love in a Village* was the first example, "a species of entertainment that has never yet appeared properly on this side of the water."[3]

The American Company's increasing emphasis on music is reflected in a Williamsburg playbill for May 1, 1771, announcing a performance of *Love in a Village* with the orchestra to be conducted by Mr. Hallam. The fact that other bills elsewhere featured Hallam as conductor of the orchestra indicates the extent—or growth—of his musical ability and the expansion of the company's instrumental resources.[4]

There were professional musicians in Virginia who may have played in the orchestra, the term then coming into use in place of "the Band of Musick" or merely "the Musick." Two instrumentalists present in Williamsburg who may have arrived with the company were William Attwood, who advertised as a teacher of French horn, hautboy, and German flute, and Francis Russworm, who taught violin and German and common flutes.[5]

Among the musicians already established in Virginia were the Italian-born Francis Alberti, Jefferson's violin teacher, "who came over with the players," taught and gave concerts, and died in Richmond in 1785, and a German, Charles Leonard, "an excellent but capricious" violinist, who was an old friend and music teacher of the Lees of Stratford Hall. Leonard died in Williamsburg in 1776, playing "his last solo" at the house of Blovet Pasteur, where Sarah Hallam, the estranged wife of Lewis Hallam, Jr., kept a dancing school. Mrs. Hallam in the 1771 Williamsburg performance of *Love in a Village* was cast as one of the singing servants in the scene of the statute or hiring fair.[6]

[38]

If Ever I'm Catch'd

sung in

LOVE IN A VILLAGE

A Comic Opera by Isaac Bickerstaffe

Isaac Bickerstaffe (ca. 1735–1812) *William Boyce (1710–1779)*

(**Moderato**)

p legato

mp

If ev - er I'm catch'd in the re - gions of Smoak, That

p

6 6/5 ♯

Seat of con - fu - sion_ and_ Noise,_____ May I ne'er know the sweets of a

6 6 ♯ ♯ 6

Slum - ber un - broke, nor the Plea - sures the Coun-try en - joys, The
Plea - sures the Coun-try en - joys.
mf
Nay, more, let them take me, to
mp
pun - ish my Sin, where gap - ing the Cock-neys they fleece, Clap me
f
mf
up with their Mon - sters, Cry "Mas-ters, walk in!" And show me for two pence a -

AT the close of the opera, when the romantic difficulties of the two young couples have been resolved and a double wedding planned, Squire Hawthorne is invited to join the party which will accompany the newlyweds to London. The usually agreeable Hawthorne replies that he will go to the church "to see the young Folks married—but as to London!—I beg to be excused." His song then echoes a sentiment—all too familiar today—that was first expressed in a seventeenth-century air: "Ah, how I abhor the Tumult and Smoke of the Town."[1]

William Boyce, the distinguished English composer, had written the music selected for the song. The original Hawthorne was John Beard, the noted tenor, who had become manager of Covent Garden Theatre in 1761, on the death of his father-in-law, John Rich. Several years later, about the time the opera was first presented in the colonies, both Beard and Boyce, plagued by an infirmity dreaded by all musicians, were forced into retirement by increasing deafness.[2]

Bickerstaffe's comic opera became a colonial favorite. Editions of both text and music were immediately and widely available. The books of the opera, sold at Covent Garden the night of the opening performance, could be had at the Williamsburg Printing Office a year and a half later. Numerous editions with the music for voice and instruments were published over the next several years. In 1770 and 1771, when the American Company presented the play in Williamsburg, the *Virginia Gazette* advertised the music for harpsichord, voice, German flute, violin, or guitar. The following year Donald Campbell of Norfolk asked St. George Tucker of Williamsburg to get him *Love in a Village*, "with the notes," from Alexander Purdie, one of the publishers of the *Virginia Gazette*. Councilor Robert Carter of Nomini Hall, in a letter written July 11, 1770, to Messrs. Hyndman and Lancaster of London, ordered along with other music "the opera call'd *Love in a Village* and musick to the same."[3]

The songs were published in a great number of single-sheet copies in London and Dublin until as late as 1790, and several were reprinted in the magazines.

[39]

Ally Croaker

sung in

THE BUCK, or THE ENGLISHMAN IN PARIS

A Comedy by Samuel Foote

[?] *Samuel Foote (1720–1777)* *Unidentified*

2

This artless young man just come from the schoolary,
A novice in love, and all its foolery,
Too dull for a wit, too grave for a joker,
And thus the gentle youth bespoke her,
Will you marry me, &c.

3

He drank with the father, he talk'd with the mother,
He romp'd with the sister, he gam'd with the brother;
He gam'd, 'til he pawned his coat to the broker,
Which cost him the heart of his dear Ally Croaker,
Oh! the fickle, fickle Ally Croaker,
Oh! the fickle Ally, Ally Croaker.

4

To all ye young men who are fond of gaming,
Who are spending your money, whilst others are saving,
Fortune's a jilt, the de'il may choke her,
A jilt more inconstant than dear Ally Croaker;
Oh! the inconstant Ally Croaker,
Oh! the inconstant Ally, Ally Croaker.

LUCINDA (with a Song) by Miss Hallam" was featured on the Williamsburg playbill for the first known performance of this farce in the colonies. On May 1, 1771, the American Company gave Foote's little comedy of a wealthy young profligate "transported to Paris by way of mending his manners" as the afterpiece to *Love in a Village*.[1]

Through the display of Lucinda's talents for singing and dancing, the Subtles, self-appointed custodians of the girl and her fortune, scheme to entrap the affections of the young buck. They allow him to watch undetected while Lucinda receives voice instruction from her singing master, Gamut.[2]

"Take care of your expression, let your eyes and address accompany the sound and the sentiment," he admonishes her.

"But, dear Gamut," implores Lucy, "if I am out, don't interrupt me, correct me afterward."

The opportunity for a song was an important part of the role, which Foote had written for Maria Macklin. Charles Macklin, Foote's acting mentor, had spared no expense in making his daughter one of the most accomplished women in England. She performed the part with "much elegance," accompanying herself on the guitar, "a new instrument," with which, as Lucinda, she is quite enchanted: "'tis so languishing, and so portable, and so soft, and so silly."[3]

The lines were among the gibes that Foote, gifted with brilliant wit and mimicry, directed at the foibles and idiosyncrasies of his time. His target was the fashionable addiction then prevalent among the young ladies to the "English" guitar, recently introduced from the Continent. Its rising popularity extended across the Atlantic; a portrait in the possession of the Virginia Historical Society shows a young lady of the colony, Lucy Randolph Burwell, playing the instrument. The musically endowed Miss Hallam should have had no difficulty in accompanying herself in Lucinda's song.[4]

At least two colonial teachers of the guitar were associated with the theatre: Giovanni Gualdo, who taught in Virginia and later led an orchestra in Philadelphia, and Thomas Wall, the singing actor, whose public offers to teach the guitar and mandolin marked the route of the American Company through the colonies.[5]

"Ally Croaker" apparently was an old tune to which the play gave new currency. It appeared in the *Universal Magazine* in the same month that Maria Macklin sang it in a Drury Lane performance of *The Englishman in Paris*, several months after the play's opening at Covent Garden. The song is mentioned by Young Wilding in Foote's *The Liar* (1762) and by Squire Hardcastle in *She Stoops to Conquer* (1773). In George Colman's *The Jealous Wife* (1761) Sir Harry Beagle sings it. The last two plays were in the colonial repertoire.[6]

[40]

Dear Heart, What a Terrible Life Am I Led

sung in

THE PADLOCK

A Comic Opera by Isaac Bickerstaffe

Isaac Bickerstaffe (ca. 1735–1812) *Charles Dibdin (1745–1814)*

mf
Dear Heart, dear
Heart, what a ter - ri - ble Life am I led; Dear Heart, dear
Heart, what a ter - ri - ble Life am I led. A dog, a dog, a dog, has a
bet - ter A dog, a dog, a dog has a bet - ter, has a bet - ter that's shel - ter'd and

fed. Night and Day 'tis the same, my Pain is their Game; Night and
Day 'tis the same, my Pain is their Game; I wish to my heart I was
dead, I wish to my heart I was dead. Night and
pp
Day 'tis the same, my Pain is their Game, Night and Day 'tis the same, my

Pain is their Game, I wish to my heart I was dead, I
wish to my heart I was dead. What e'ers to be
done? what e'ers to be done? Poor
Black must run! Poor Black must
f
mp

run. Mun-go here, Mun-go there, Mun-go
f
mp
ev' - ry where! Mun-go ev' - ry where! A - bove and be - low, Sir-rah, come, Sir-rah, go! A -
bove and be - low, do so, and do so! Oh! Oh! Oh! Oh! What a
f p f p
ter - ri - ble Life_ am I led! Oh! Oh! Oh! Oh! What a
f p f p
6

ter - ri - ble Life am I led. Night and Day 'tis the same, my
Pain is their Game, Night and Day 'tis the same, my Pain is their Game. I
wish to my heart I was dead! dead! dead!, I
wish to my heart I was dead! dead! dead! I

LEWIS HALLAM, Jr., as Mungo in colonial performances of *The Padlock*, the most popular of Bickerstaffe's musical plays, scored a tremendous hit as the comic servant who sings this song in protest against his treatment by his employer Don Diego.[1]

The elderly Don Diego has agreed with the parents of Leonora to keep her properly chaperoned on his estate while he observes her temper and conduct to see if she will make him a suitable wife. He orders Mungo to guard his house while he is away and, on threat of severe punishment, to permit no one to enter.

A picture of the scene, the fifth in Act I—in which Mungo sings the song—shows Charles Dibdin, the composer of the music and the originator of the role, standing at the entry to Don Diego's house. Its windows are barred and its iron grate padlocked. Beneath is printed a line from the song: "I wish to me Heart me was Dead! Dead! Dead!" The picture was published in London in 1769, the same year that the comic opera became one of the most popular additions to the colonial repertoire.[2]

Hallam's success in the role was attributed to his study of the native characteristics and dialect in Jamaica. A Philadelphia admirer in 1772 called him "the best Mungo upon the British stage," a tribute usually reserved for Dibdin. The Philadelphian was not as generous in his comment on the performance of Thomas Wall in his role of Leander, who courts Leonora disguised as a wandering guitar player: "We verily believe Mr. Wall does as well as he can therefore we must not censure him."[3]

Dibdin was only twenty-three years old when he composed the music for *The Padlock*. Its songs gained widespread popularity as concert numbers and were issued in single-sheet copies and reprinted in periodicals. Four months before *The Padlock* made its first American appearance the text of one of its songs, sung by Ursula, the maid-chaperone, was printed in the Poet's Corner of the *Virginia Gazette* under the title "A New Song," but not identified with the play.[4]

When a Williamsburg playbill announced a performance of *The Padlock* for May 2, 1771, the "musick" for the opera already had been advertised in the *Virginia Gazette*. The following August it again was offered for sale "for Harpsichord, Voice, German Flute, Violin, or Guitar."[5]

The play also retained its popularity. A planned performance of *The Padlock* at Valley Forge by amateur actors of the American army had to be cancelled when the British evacuated Philadelphia and the Americans moved to occupy the city.[6] Performances of the opera still were being given in the nineteenth century.

[41]

Ye Mortals Whom Fancies and Troubles Perplex

sung in

LETHE, or AESOP IN THE SHADES

A Comedy by David Garrick

David Garrick (1717–1779) *Unidentified*

2

Old Maids shall forget what they wish'd for in vain,
And young ones, the Rover they cannot regain;
The Rake shall forget how last night he was cloy'd,
And Chloe again be with Passion enjoy'd.
Obey then the Summons, to Lethe repair,
And drink an Oblivion to Trouble and Care.

3

The Wife at one Draught may forget all her Wants,
Or drench her fond Fool, to forget her Gallants.
The troubl'd in mind shall go chearful away,
And yesterday's Wretch be quite happy today.
Obey then the Summons, to Lethe repair,
And drink an Oblivion to Trouble and Care.

DAVID GARRICK'S first play amusingly caricatured his fashionable contemporaries in the pattern of Vanbrugh's *Aesop* of 1696.[1] In the opening scene Mercury and Aesop are waiting near the river Lethe for Charon to ferry across to them a group of mortals coming for judgment on their past follies. "Lest the Solemnity of the Place strike 'em with too much Dread, I'll raise Musick," Mercury tells Aesop, and he sings this song. Charon's passengers are far from being overcome by either dread or remorse. After they have preened and boasted and criticized, Aesop decides "'Tis vain to reason with such Beings," and tells Mercury to dismiss them to Earth as happy as Lethe can make them.[2]

Garrick, under an assumed name, made his acting debut in *Lethe* at a provincial theatre in Ipswich shortly before his sensational appearance as Richard III at Goodman's Fields on October 19, 1741. He frequently revised the play, which was a favorite afterpiece with both author and audiences, including those in colonial America, to keep it topical and in conformity with changing tastes. In 1749 William Boyce composed music for two songs in *Lethe*; this may be one of them.[3]

The first colonial performance was given by Robert Upton's company, "that Sett of Pretenders" that Upton, the Hallam's perfidious advance agent, had formed from part of the Murray-Kean group. Only four years after Garrick had assumed the management of Drury Lane, his fame was such that the New York advertisement stated that the play was a "Dramatick Entertainment wrote by the celebrated Mr. Garrick."[4]

The Hallam Company on its arrival billed the afterpiece as a "Dramatic Satyre," the author's own designation of it in the 1749 edition. Forty years later Lewis Hallam, Jr., inaccurately recalled *Lethe* instead of *The Anatomist* as the afterpiece to *The Merchant of Venice* at the company's opening performance in Williamsburg.[5] As one of the company's popular afterpieces, it probably was given there at a repeat performance of the mainpiece later in the season.

The Hallam Company's singer, William Adcock, had the role of Mercury in which John Beard, the tenor, was featured at Drury Lane. In 1762, Sturt, an actor who undertook vocal parts in the American Company, played Mercury. Presumably he was the actor of the same name who had played minor roles at Drury Lane and in the summer theatres at Twickenham and Richmond during the 1750s. After 1767 Stephen Woolls was assigned the role, which was billed as "Mercury, with Songs."[6]

[42]

She Walks as She Dreams

sung in

ALEXANDER THE GREAT, or THE RIVAL QUEENS

A Tragedy by Nathaniel Lee

Nathaniel Lee (1653–1692) — *Daniel Purcell (ca. 1660–1717)*

mp
She walks as she dreams in a
pp rit.
a tempo p
Gar - den of Flow'rs, And her Hands are em - ploy'd in the beau - ti - ful
Bow'rs; She dreams of the Man that is far from the Grove, And
6
all her soft Fan - cy still runs on her Love; All, all her soft
6 6 ♮ 4

Fan - cy still runs on her Love. She nods — o'er the Brooks that run
purl - ing — a - long, And the Night - in - gales lull
her most
fast with a Song; They lull

AMONG the "few great beauties" that Colley Cibber conceded were to be found in the "furious Fustian and turgid Rant" of Nathaniel Lee's play, he must have included this song.[1] It is a portion of the operatic dialogue that opens Act V. Statira, the second wife of the "fatal glory of the world, the headlong Alexander," is discovered asleep in the bower of Semiramis, legendary queen of Babylon. The spirits of her mother, Queen Statira, and her father, the Persian King Darius conquered by Alexander, stand on either side with daggers poised. Their song warns of the doom which the gods have decreed. Before the tragedy ends Statira is fatally stabbed by the jealous Roxana, first wife of Alexander.

The play was Lee's greatest dramatic success. An eloquent but too-nervous actor turned playwright, he wrote of himself in the dedication to another of his tragedies, *Theodosius, or The Force of Love*, that he "abounded in ungoverned fancy." In the ten years before his complete mental derangement in 1684, he supplied the stage with many plays from which contemporary music publishers reprinted the songs. Some of these were still to be found in the collections of the next century.[2]

His tragedy was an "opera" in the sense of the times; performances of it were billed "with the vocal and instrumental music essential to the play." Although never without its detractors, the drama was revived frequently.

Daniel Purcell set music to the dialogue song for a revival sometime before 1701.[3]

Another revival of *Alexander the Great* was given in 1764 at Drury Lane, while Garrick, who disliked it, was traveling abroad. A critic castigated it as having been written in "that Period when Dryden and Lee produced the Dramatick Monsters called Heroic Plays and Tragedies in Rime" and as containing the character of a "mad Hero drawn by a mad Poet." He was impressed, however, with the "magnificence of the Triumphal Entry into Babylon," and thought it conducted "with great propriety." This adornment with its choral singing and instrumental accompaniment always was a drawing card, as was the bower scene in which the dialogue was sung.[4]

The tragedy was performed for the first time in America during the 1768–69 season in Philadelphia and New York. It remained in the American Company's repertoire for the rest of the colonial period. Although no performance has been recorded on the Virginia-Maryland circuit, it probably was given during one of the later tours of the company in that area. It may also have been one of the plays given in Williamsburg's first theatre.[5]

The American Company had acquired the resources for the vocal and instrumental parts as early as 1762, when it staged Lee's *Theodosius*. The ghost scene in *Alexander the Great* could have drawn upon any of the singing members of the company with the exception of Miss Hallam, who, as Statira, was on stage.[6]

[43]

No Ice so Hard, so Cold, as I

sung in

MISS IN HER TEENS, or MEDLEY OF LOVERS

A Comedy by David Garrick

David Garrick (1717–1779) *Thomas A. Arne* (1710–1778)

cold as I, 'til warm'd and soft - - en'd by your Eye; And
now my Heart dis-solves a - - way in dreams by Night, in Sighs by Day.
Now my Heart dis - - solves a - way, dis- solves
a - way, in Dreams by Night, in Sighs by Day, in

dreams by Night, in Sighs by Day. No bru-tal Pas-sion
fires my Breast, which loathes the Ob-ject, loathes the Ob-ject when poss-ess'd, But
one of bound - - less gen - - tle kind whose Joys, whose Joys are
cen-ter'd in the Mind, in the Mind in the Mind. Then
rit.
andante
a tempo

take with me Love's bet-ter, bet-ter past, Take with me Love's
bet-ter, bet-ter part, his dow - - - ny Wing, his dow - - - ny Wing, but
not, not his Dart, no, not his Dart. Take with me Love's bet-ter part, Love's bet-ter
part, Love's bet - ter part, his dow - - - - - - - - - - - - - -
f
p
6 4 5 3
8 6 7
6
7

- ny, dow - ny Wing but not his Dart,
not his Dart.
Take with
(allarg.)
me his dow - ny Wing, but not, not his Dart, no, not his
Dart, no, not his dart.

"THE Tune is nothing, the Manner's all," says Fribble as he prepares to sing the verses that he has just read to Miss Biddy Bellair. Laughing at her foppish suitor, she protests that they are very pretty but that she doesn't understand them. "These light pieces are never so well understood in Reading as in Singing," Fribble explains. "I have set 'em myself, and will endeavour to give them to you—la!—la!—I have an abominable cold, and can't sing a note. . . ."

Fribble's attempt at a song takes place in Act II of *Miss in Her Teens*, first performed at Covent Garden in 1747. It became one of the most popular afterpieces on the colonial stage with nearly three dozen performances recorded, including that by the Virginia Company in Williamsburg on April 6, 1768. Undoubtedly it was given in all the other theatre seasons in Virginia's capital from 1751 to 1773.[1]

"Overcharged with wit and humour" after a recovery from illness, David Garrick wrote the play with the part of the ridiculous Fribble designed for himself. Audiences found his role, in which he mimicked "eleven Men of Fashion," vastly entertaining. There was jest in the fact that Fribble's song was expressly written for Garrick, who, as his contemporaries agreed, had no ear for music.[2]

Arne's setting, a parody of the *agitato* operatic style with the accompaniment as breathless as the air, may not have been the original setting. James Dodd, a former strolling player who shone in coxcomb parts, was billed as Fribble, "with a new Song" at Drury Lane on April 25, 1766. Whether this setting of the song was new for Dodd or new for the text is not determined. Possibly Arne was the original composer and made a new setting at this time. He had been composing for the theatres and for Garrick as early as the first performance of *Miss in Her Teens* twenty years before.[3]

The first known Fribble in the colonies was John Singleton, the actor-violinist with the Hallam Company. One of his successors in the role was Thomas Wall, the hard-working comedian-singer, who joined the American Company in 1765 and was still theatrically active in America after the Revolution. Another Fribble was Adam Allyn, a singer and actor with the American Company from 1759 until his death in 1768 in New York. Later that year the play was given as a benefit performance for the Storer sisters. In a conceit borrowed from abroad, Maria, the youngest, played Fribble, with her sister Fannie as the blustering Captain Flash. Nearly twenty years earlier their mother had "attempted" the role of Fribble at the Smock Alley Theatre in Dublin.[4] All the colonial Fribbles appeared in other singing roles.

[44]

The Tragical History of the Life and Death of Billy Pringle's Pig

sung in

THE MAYOR OF GARRAT

A Comedy by Samuel Foote

Samuel Foote (1720–1777) — *Francesco Geminiani (1687–1762)*

2

Billy Pringle—he
Sat down and cry'd,
Betty Pringle—she
Lay down and died.
So there was an End
Of One, Two, Three,
Betty Pringle, Billy Pringle,
And PIGGY WIGGEY.

SAMUEL FOOTE'S comic afterpiece concerning the election of the slow-witted, hen-pecked Jerry Sneak as village mayor was added to the colonial repertoire in 1767, and performed by the Virginia-New American Company in 1768 and 1769. However, Sneak's tragical song could not have been heard in Williamsburg before the spring of 1772, during the American Company's final tour of Virginia. The first notice of its introduction into *The Mayor of Garrat*, eight years after the play's first performance, appeared on September 13, 1771, when the bill at Foote's theatre in the Haymarket announced that Thomas Weston as Sneak would sing "Johnny Pringle," the "last new favourite Song."[1]

The song, which in later versions sometimes identified the pig's owner as Billy (as in the 1780 edition used here) or as Betty Pringle, was not printed in the comedy, although it became an accepted part of it. Foote's habit of changing his plays at will to satirize some topical event or timely bit of gossip meant constant deviations in performance that never emerged in the printed editions.[2]

Foote had written the role of Jerry Sneak for Thomas Weston, a comedian who could look and play the fool while appearing completely oblivious to an audience's laughter. Weston must have introduced the song during Sneak's conversation with Major Sturgeon in which he says [in the printed text], "I myself have learned to sing 'An Old Woman Cloath'd in Gray' but I durst not sing out loud because my wife would overhear me, and she says I bawl worser than the Broom-man." Weston's rendition of the song, which became a permanent and popular part of his role, would have been a bid for further laughter, his lack of voice being well known.[3]

The reason for the introduction of this particular song is difficult to discover now. The verses first appeared in *Mother Goose's Melody* between 1760 and 1765. Because of Foote's known antipathy to doctors both individually and collectively, it may be that the song, or at least its title, was directed at the very distinguished Sir John Pringle, a physician to the king's household, who was elected president of the Royal Society in 1772, the year following the song's first appearance in the play.[4]

The Johnny (or Billy) Pringle song was set to a "Favourite Minuet" by Francesco Geminiani, an eminent Italian violinist and widely known composer who resided in London after 1714. The composer was referred to as "Jimmy Nanny" in a satirical sketch of the frivolities of the fashionable younger set, which the *Virginia Gazette* reprinted in 1737 from a London periodical.[5]

The minuet had been provided with a song text as early as 1729, when it was published in *The Musical Miscellany* as "Gently Touch the warbling Lyre," the "words by Mr. Bradley." Picked up by the ballad-opera arrangers, the tune served for Air 9 in *The Beau in the Suds* and for Air 13 in *Don Quixote in England*. In the latter farce Henry Fielding anticipated Foote by thirty years in having fun with an election.[6] Both ballad operas were given on the colonial stage.

Jerry Sneak's role in the colonies was played by two actors, either of whom could have been seen in it during their appearances in Williamsburg with the American Company. Thomas Wall, often cast in comic and singing roles, acted the part first. Perhaps he was able to pattern his performance on Weston's: He announced when he joined the American Company in 1765 that he came from the Theatre Royal in Drury Lane and the Haymarket in London, so he may have been at the first performance of the play. The year after Weston was first recorded as singing "Johnny Pringle" at the Haymarket, the fifty-three-year-old Owen Morris took the role in Philadelphia. Morris, considered unrivaled in jest and buffoonery, was a non-singer who could have given the pig's tragic history its properly ludicrous effect.[7]

[45]

Attend, All Ye Fair

sung in

THE WAY TO KEEP HIM

A Comedy by Arthur Murphy

Arthur Murphy (*1727–1805*) *Attributed to* ______ *Smith*

2

When Juno accepted the cestus* of love,
She at first was but handsome, charming became;
It taught her with skill the soft passions to move,
To kindle at once and to keep up the flame.

3

'Tis this magic secret gives th' eyes all their fire,
Lends the voice melting accents, impassions the kiss;
Gives the mouth the sweet smiles that 'waken desire,
And plants round the fair each incentive to bliss.

4

Thence flows the gay chat, more than reason that charms,
The eloquent blush, that can beauty improve;
The fond sigh, the fond vow, the soft touch that alarms
The tender disdain, the renewal of love.

5

Ye fair, take the cestus, and practice its art;
The mind unaccomplish'd, mere features are vain;
Exert your sweet power, you conquer each heart,
And the Loves, Joys, and Graces walk in your train.

*A girdle that gives the wearer the power of attracting love.

TO her own accompaniment on the harpsichord, Mrs. Bellmour, a young widow "of great beauty and fashion," sings this song for "Lord Etheridge," the suitor who visits her surreptitiously in a sedan chair with "the curtains drawn close about his ears." The widow compliments him on his authorship of the song and tells him he is a "regular Vauxhall Poet . . . . Come, you shall hear how I murder it. I have no voice today, but you shall hear me."

The scene leads to the realization by the widow and Mrs. Lovemore, waiting in the next room, that "Lord Etheridge" is the latter's philandering husband. The two ladies unite to turn the tables, and "the gay, the florid, the magnifique Lord Etheridge dwindles down to plain Mr. Lovemore, the married man."

The play and its song were first introduced to Virginians in 1760 in the pages of two English periodicals. The *Gentleman's Magazine* printed the song text, as well as "some account of the last new comedy call'd *The Way to Keep Him* by A. Murphy," and the *Universal Magazine* printed the song with the music the same year.[1]

The comedy was performed in Williamsburg on April 28, 1772, with *The Oracle* as its afterpiece. It is probable that it had been played there earlier by the Virginia

Company in 1768, with Mrs. Osborne singing the song as the Widow Bellmour. The role was taken by Nancy Hallam in the American Company's performances.[2]

The play was one of seven in the colonial repertoire written by Arthur Murphy, the Anglo-Irish lawyer and playwright.[3] At its first performance in 1759 at Drury Lane the musically talented Maria Macklin played the widow.

A composer identified only as "Smith" provided the setting for her song. Of the many Smiths associated with eighteenth-century music and theatre, this particular one probably was Adam Smith, an English singer and song-writer connected with the Grotto Gardens, St. George's Fields, in 1771.[4]

When Murphy's play was expanded to five acts in 1762, Arne set an additional song for his sister, Mrs. Cibber, as the Widow Bellmour. The song text, printed at the end of the play in later editions, was written by David Garrick, who, according to Murphy, believed that the relationship of song to a good play was that of horse-radish to a dish of Old English roast beef.[5]

[46]

Would You with Her You Love Be Blest

sung in

THE ORACLE

A Comedy translated from the French

Translated by Susannah Cibber (1714–1766) *Thomas A. Arne (1710–1778)*

love be blest, Ye Lo - vers_ these in - struc - tions mind,
con-ceal the Pas - sion_ in_ your_ Breast; Be
dumb, in - sen - si - ble,
in - sen - si - ble and blind.
Be dumb, be dumb, in - sen - si - ble and blind.
p
f

But if with gen - tle
looks you meet, And see the art - less blush - - es rise, Be
si - lent, lov - ing, and dis - creet, The
O - ra-cle no more im - plies, The O - ra-cle no more im - plies.

2

When once you prove the Maid sincere,
  Where Virtue is with Beauty join'd,
Then boldly let yourself appear
  No more insensible, or blind;
Pour forth the transports of your Heart,
  And speak your Soul without disguise;
'Tis fondness, fondness must impart,
  The Oracle no more implies.

3

Tho' pleasing, fatal is the Snare
  That still entraps all Womankind;
Ladies, beware, be wise, take Care,
  Be deaf, insensible, and blind;
But shou'd some fond deserving Youth
  Agree to join in Hymen's ties,
Be tender, constant, crown his Truth—
  The Oracle no more implies.

SUSANNAH CIBBER translated this little afterpiece from the French and presented it as *The Oracle* at Covent Garden in 1752. As the author and leading actress, in the role of Cinthia, she brought the play to its conclusion with this song,[1] then spoke the epilogue. In it she observed that "a girl that's in her teens by instinct knows that men are not machines. . . ."

Cinthia has made this discovery in the course of the play. The Fairy Queen has sequestered the girl from all knowledge of other mortals as part of her plan to avert the prophecy made by the oracle at the birth of her son Oberon. To prevent the misfortunes threatening him, Cinthia must be induced to fall in love with Oberon believing him to be as "deaf, dumb, and insensible" as the animated statues that are her servants. The complications occur when Oberon balks at his robot role, and Cinthia begins to doubt that the little birds she sees are machines like her harpsichord and lute. "I can't say I ever once thought of kissing my Harpsichord or minding whether my Lute was hot or cold."

Eventually all is happily resolved, and the Fairy Queen bids her son to be a tender, complaisant, and affectionate husband and thereby "prove a contrast to the times," advice which may have reflected the author's unhappy marriage to the unprincipled Theophilus Cibber, actor son of Colley. Mrs. Cibber was the younger sister of Thomas Arne, who composed the music for her play. An actress and contralto singer, she had the approbation and sympathy of London audiences.[2]

The first record of the play in Williamsburg was a notice by the American Company in the *Virginia Gazette* in 1772 of a "Comedy (never perform'd before) call'd *The Way to Keep Him* . . . to which will be added *The Oracle*."[3]

At least one member of the American Company had played in *The Oracle* before coming to the colonies. Mrs. John Henry, the former Ann Storer, elder sister of Maria, had taken part in the play at Sheridan's Smock Alley Theatre in Dublin in 1758 when "all the Characters [were] to be perform'd by Mrs. Storer's children," one of whom, "Miss Storer," played Cinthia with the "original Epilogue."[4]

The afterpiece had taken its place in the colonial repertoire in 1766 in Charleston, where it was described as the "most delicate, sensible, petite piece on the English stage." Nancy Hallam played Cinthia "with a song incident to the piece." A few years later a colonial admirer compared her voice to that of the author: "I thought I heard once more the warblings of Cibber in my ear."[5]

In December 1767 Miss Hallam played "Cinthia with a Song" when *The Oracle*, *Richard III*, and a harlequin pantomime ballet were given by command of New York's Governor Sir Henry Moore for the entertainment of a party of Indian warriors from South Carolina.[6]

[47]

Long Have I Been with Grief Opprest

sung in

THE FEMALE PARSON, or THE BEAU IN THE SUDS

A Ballad Opera by Charles Coffey

Charles Coffey (d. 1745) *Unidentified*

TWENTY years after Charles Coffey's ballad farce failed in London, the theatre group that preceded the Hallams successfully revived it in the colonies. The actors, under the management of Walter Murray and Thomas Kean, performed it between 1750 and 1752 in New York and Maryland. In New York they played it at least five times between March 12, 1750, and June 27, 1751, and in Annapolis twice in July 1752. The farce, as one of their stock afterpieces, also must have been given in Virginia, where they played in the interval between the New York and Maryland seasons, having opened their new theatre in Williamsburg in October 1751.[1]

The music had proved more popular than the play, and after its failure Coffey, salvaging what he could, published the songs with their tunes the same year.[2]

This song is sung by Lady Quibus, whose release from an unwanted and unconsummated marriage to Sir Quibble Quibus, "an old Debauch'd Justice of the Peace," is the subject of the plot. The "female parson" is Pinner, her maid, who, disguised as a preacher, performed what is discovered to be the fraudulent nuptials.

The tune was an old one that William Thompson adapted to "Love's Goddess in a Myrtle Grove," with verses by the Scottish poet Allan Ramsay, for Thompson's collection *Orpheus Caledonius* in 1725. The words and music of the song were reprinted by John Watts in his *Musical Miscellany* in 1729 and in other collections.[3]

No cast has been found for either the London or the colonial presentations. The latter were given under the farce's alternative title, *The Beau in the Suds*.[4]

[48]

The Romp's Song

sung in

THE PROVOK'D HUSBAND, or THE JOURNEY TO LONDON

A Comedy by Sir John Vanbrugh and Colley Cibber

Henry Carey (ca. 1687–1743) *Henry Carey*

2

My Mother, she says I'm too coming,
And still in my Ears she is drumming,
And still in my Ears she is drumming
That I such vain Thoughts shou'd shun.
My Sisters, they cry O bye! O fye!
  And yet I can see
  They're as coming as me;
So let me have Husbands in plenty!
I'd rather have twenty times twenty
Than die an Old Maid undone.

THE supposedly guileless Jenny, her mind full of a masquerade planned for the morrow, sings this song while the bogus Count Bassett, scheming to marry her for her money, attempts to arrange a compromising rendezvous.

Jenny and her family, the country cousins visiting London, were part of the subplot of the comedy that the dramatist-architect Sir John Vanbrugh had not finished when he died in 1726. Colley Cibber, associate manager of Drury Lane, completed the play and produced it on January 10, 1728. Cibber confounded his enemies by leading them to believe that the portions of the play they so much admired were Vanbrugh's and eventually revealing that they were his. The play's run of twenty-eight nights, although in competition with Gay's *The Beggar's Opera*, came to an end only because of the exhaustion of the celebrated Mrs. Oldfield, who played the extravagant and frivolous Lady Townley. Cibber's daughter-in-law, Jennie Johnson, Theophilus Cibber's first wife, created the role of Jenny.[1]

Jenny's song, with words and music by Henry Carey, proved so popular that another, for which Carey also provided the words and music, was added to the part in Act V. The following April the play was announced "with the Romp's Song as usual and a new Ballad call'd The Fine Lady's Life to be sung in the Character of Miss

Jenny."[2] Nearly half a century later David Garrick, in his comedy *The Irish Widow*, also seen on the colonial stage, had the Widow Brady sing "The Romp's Song."[3]

Two years after Cibber's death in 1757 his granddaughter, Catherine Maria Harman, appeared as Jenny in *The Provok'd Husband* in her first colonial season in Philadelphia. The comedy, one of the most popular on the American stage, had been performed in the colonies at least since the Murray-Kean enterprise in the early 1750s. The only dated Virginia performances were on April 22, 1772 in Williamsburg, with *Thomas and Sally* as the afterpiece, and in May of the preceding year in Fredericksburg.[4]

Nancy Hallam, one of the company's leading actress-singers, usually played the role of Jenny after 1765, but the Fredericksburg playbill shows Maria Storer in the part. She may also have played it in Williamsburg earlier in the spring, if, as was likely, the comedy was performed during the company's season there.

Virginians may have laughed with others at the gibes directed at Colley Cibber by Pope in the *Dunciad* and by others after Cibber became laureate, but they enjoyed his plays. Of those given on the colonial stage, including *The Careless Husband*, *Love Makes a Man*, *She Wou'd and She Wou'd Not*, and *The Schoolboy*, by far the most popular were *Damon and Phillida* and *The Provok'd Husband*.

[49]

The Echoing Horn

sung in

THOMAS AND SALLY, or THE SAILOR'S RETURN

An Opera by Isaac Bickerstaffe

Isaac Bickerstaffe (ca. 1735–1812) *Thomas A. Arne (1710–1778)*

With spirit

f

p

f

tr

tr

tr

The Ech - o - ing Horn calls the Sports-man a - broad, To
Horse! my brave Boys, and a - way! The Morn-ing is up, and the Cry of the

Hounds up - braids our too te - dious de - lay. What Plea - sures we
feel in pur - su - ing the Fox, O'er Hill and o'er Val - ley he flies.
Then fol - low, we'll soon o - ver-take him, Huz - za! The Trai - tor is
seiz'd and he dies! He dies,

2

Triumphant returning at Night with the spoil
   Like Bacchanals shouting and gay,
How sweet with a Bottle and Lass to refresh
   And lose the fatigues of the Day.
With Sport, Love, and Wine, fickle Fortune defye
   Dull Wisdom and Happiness sours,
Since Life is no more than a Passage at best,
   Let's strew the Way over with Flow'rs;
Since Life, etc.

THE "enchanting Notes" of "The Echoing Horn," the opening number in Arne's little opera *Thomas and Sally*, echoed one summer evening in Williamsburg in 1769 for the pleasure of Baron de Botetourt, next-to-last royal governor of Virginia.

A letter Anne Blair, daughter of the Honorable John Blair, wrote to her sister Mrs. Braxton, quotes the refrain to the second stanza of the song in this delightful glimpse of domestic music in the colony:

> Mrs. Dawson's Family stay'd the Evening with us, and the Coach was at the door to carry them Home, by ten o'clock; but every one appearing in great Spirits, it was proposed to set at the Step's and Sing a few Song's, which was no sooner said then done; while thus we were employ'd, a Candle & Lanthorn was observed to be coming up Street (except Polly Clayton censuring their ill taste, for having a Candle such a fine Night)—no one took any notice of it—till we saw, who ever it was, stop't to listen to our enchanting Notes—each Warbler was immeadiately silenced; whereupon, the invader to our Melody, call'd out in a most rapturous Voice, Charming! Charming! proceed for God sake, or I go Home directly—no sooner were these words utter'd, then all as with one consent sprung from their Seats, and the Air eccho'd with pray Walk in my Lord; No—indeed he would not, he would set on the Step's too;

> so after a few ha, ha, ha's, and being told what all knew—that it was a delightfull Evening, at his desire we strew'd the way over with Flowers—&c. &c. till a full half hour was elaps'd, when all retir'd to their respective Homes.[1]

The flower-strewing song is part of the entry music for the squire and his hunting party, in which clarinets and horns echo each other in a manner borrowed from the Germans. In the plot the huntsman squire has game in view other than the four-footed species when he tries to persuade Sally, the sweetheart of Thomas the absent sailor, that "morals are for gray beards." Despite the persuasions of the older Dorcas, who tells her that "the Mayday of Life is for pleasure," Sally remains unconvinced. Soon Thomas comes home from the sea to drive off the thwarted squire and claim his bride.

Thomas and Sally was a true miniature opera using recitative rather than spoken dialogue. In it, clarinets were used for the first time in an English opera orchestra. It was the third in order of popularity of Bickerstaffe's plays.[2]

By the time of the play's first performance in the colonies at Philadelphia in 1766, the American Company could muster the horns and, at least in some areas on its circuit, the clarinets for the entry music. Among the professional French horn players known to have been in Virginia were William Attwood, a teacher of the horn and woodwind instruments in 1771, and John Schneider (Schnyder), who had given instrumental concerts there. Two other horn players, Stotherd, also a guitarist, and Humphries, may have traveled with the company between their concert appearances in New York in 1770 and Charleston in 1773. Clarinets, although relatively new instruments in London theatre orchestras, were mentioned in connection with concerts in Philadelphia and New York as early as 1764.

A clarinetist who may have traveled with the American Company was "Mr. Hoffman, Junior," who appeared in a concert in Philadelphia with several of the company's singers. Another musician who may have played the clarinet and who would have been available to the company in Virginia was John Stadler (or Stadley), music master to several prominent families in the colony from 1766 to 1781. In some areas, the company could have drawn upon clarinetists from the military bands that occasionally assisted at the theatres in special musical accompaniments.[3]

Anne Blair's letter was written almost a year before the American Company's first recorded presentation of *Thomas and Sally* in Williamsburg on June 20, 1770, a date on which George Washington attended the theatre. But the opera almost certainly had been given there two years earlier by the Virginia-New American Company, who had it in their repertoire. On April 21, 1772, for the second recorded Williamsburg performance, the opera was the afterpiece to *The Provok'd Husband*, the same play with which it was introduced to colonial audiences.[4]

The role of the squire, originated by George Mattocks at Covent Garden, was played by Stephen Woolls in all the published casts of the fifteen known colonial performances. Woolls, considered the best male vocalist on the eighteenth-century American stage, had been a pupil of Thomas Arne, the composer of *Thomas and Sally*. His most notable appearance outside the theatre, however, occurred in Williamsburg on October 19, 1770, when, a little over a year after the singing party on the Blair steps, he conducted the anthem at the funeral of that "excellent man and so good a Governor," Lord Botetourt.[5]

[50]

Epilogue Song

sung in

THE IRISH WIDOW

A Comedy by David Garrick

David Garrick (1717–1779) *Joseph Vernon* (1738–1782)

think that she's so out of Fash - - ion, To_ mar-ry and then to be tam - - ed.
f
'Tis_ Love, the dear Joy, that old fash-ion'd Boy, Has
mp
got in my Breast with his Qui - - ver; The_ blind Ur - chin, he struck the
Cush - la - ma - chree, And a Hus-band se - cures me for - ev - - er. Ye_

2

Ye Critics to murder so willing,
Pray see all our Errors with blindness;
For once, change your method of killing,
And kill a fond Widow with kindness.
If you look so severe, in a fit of despair;
Again I shall draw forth my Steel, Sirs;
You know I've the art to be twice thro your Heart,
Before I can make you feel, Sirs.
Brother Soldiers I hope you'll protect me,
Nor let cruel Critics dissect me;
To favor my cause be but ready,
And grateful you'll find, Widow Brady.

Ye Leaders of dress and of fashion,
Who gallop post haste to your Ruin,
Whose Taste has destroy'd all your Passion,
Pray, what do you think of my wooing?
You call it damn'd low, your head and arms so,
So listless, so loose, and so lazy;
But what pray can you, that I cannot do!
O fye! my dear Creatures, be easy.
Ye Patriots and Courtiers so hearty,
To speech it and vote for your Party;
For once be both constant and steady,
And grateful you'll find, Widow Brady.

4

To all that I see here before me,
The bottom the Top and the middle;
For Music I now must implore ye
No wedding without Pipe and Fiddle.
If all are in tune, pray let it be soon,
My heart in my bosom is prancing;
If your hands shou'd unite to give us delight,
Oh, that's the best Piping & Dancing.
Your Plaudits to me are a treasure.
Your smiles are a dow'r for a Lady,
Oh, Joy to you all in full measure,
So wishes and prays Widow Brady.

THE epilogue song that concludes Garrick's comedy is sung "in Character" by the modest young Irish widow, Mrs. Brady, after she has outwitted the elderly Whittle. Smitten with her charms, Whittle has attempted to supplant his nephew, whose purse strings he holds, as the widow's fiancé. To disenchant him, the widow adopts "a fine, bold way" with "a tongue fixed so loose in her mouth" she can't stop it and with not a thought in her head but operas, plays, and masquerades.

At the end of the farce, having achieved both her purpose and the nephew, the widow addresses the audience as a preliminary to the epilogue song:[1] "By your permission, I will tell my mind to this good company, and for fear my words should want ideas, I will add an Irish tune that may carry off a bad voice . . . ."

The "Irish" tune was the work of a non-Irish composer, Joseph Vernon, actor and tenor at Drury Lane and Vauxhall Gardens, who was born in Coventry and died in London. Vernon also composed music for another epilogue song.[2]

David Garrick wrote *The Irish Widow* in a week's time to provide a new style of role for Ann Barry, who had been the bona fide Irish widow of William Dancer when she married the popular actor Spranger Barry in 1768. Mrs. Barry was not at ease in the character, but other actresses later played the part with more success.[3]

The comedy became part of the colonial company's repertoire in the last year of its existence. It was the afterpiece "never perform'd in America" to *Tamerlane* in New York on June 28, 1773, at a benefit for Mr. and Mrs. Morris, with the latter as the Widow Brady, a part she continued to play in Jamaica where the company performed during the Revolution. Her role there was billed "with the Epilogue Song."[4]

The tall, stately Charlotte Morris, the second and much younger wife of Owen Morris, was described as giving her best performances in the farces and comedies in which she had singing roles. At her death in 1826 she was the last survivor of the actors and actresses who had appeared on the stage in Virginia's colonial capital.[5]

List of Abbreviations

used in the NOTES and the BIBLIOGRAPHY

Full citation of printed works will be found in the Bibliography

Add. Mss.	Additional Manuscripts
BBB	*The British Broadside Ballad and its Music*
BM	British Museum, London
BMB	*British Musical Biography*
BU	*British Union Catalogue of Early Music Printed Before the Year 1801*
CW	Colonial Williamsburg Research Department, Williamsburg, Va.
DAB	*Dictionary of American Biography*
DNB	*Dictionary of National Biography*
ESB	*English Song Books, 1650–1702*
FL	Folger Shakespeare Library, Washington, D.C.
Grove III & V	*Grove's Dictionary of Music and Musicians*, 3rd edn. 1935; 5th edn. 1954.
HL	Henry E. Huntington Library, San Marino, Calif.
IEAHC	Institute of Early American History and Culture, Williamsburg, Va.
LC	Library of Congress, Washington, D.C.
LDA	*London Daily Advertiser*
LS	*The London Stage, 1660–1800: A Calendar . . .* (4 parts)
micro	Microfilm or microcard
ML	*Music and Letters*
MM	*The Musical Miscellany*
MQ	*Musical Quarterly*
OCEL	*Oxford Companion to English Literature*
ODNR	*Oxford Dictionary of Nursery Rhymes*
PPM	*Pills to Purge Melancholy*
RMA	Royal Music Association
s. sh. fol.	single sheet folio
VG	*Virginia Gazette* Initials in parentheses designate publishers of competing papers after 1766, as follows: (R) Rind; (PD) Purdie & Dixon; (P) Purdie; (Pi) Pinkney; (D) Dixon & Hunter, Dixon & Nicolson; (C) Clarkson & Davis
VHS	Virginia Historical Society, Richmond, Va.
VSL	Virginia State Library, Richmond, Va.
W&M	College of William and Mary, Williamsburg, Va.
W&M micro	*Three Centuries of English Drama*

Notes

AT the head of the notes for each selection will be found (to the *left*) the source of the play text and of the song text; and (to the *right*) the source of the music. The library or archival location of manuscript and other sources is given where appropriate. Full bibliographic data for generally available publications, here cited in short form, will be found in the Bibliography. Below the source information appear the dates of the first, or first known, performances in London and the colonies.

[1]
THE TRIFLE
(The Beaux' Stratagem)

Farquhar, *Four Plays*, 353–456; song text, 402–3. (Several of the verses are omitted here.)

"Sung by Archer in *The Beaux' Stratagem*." *Musical Miscellany*, IV, 100; bass given. [CW]

First performance: London, Queen's, 1707
First known American performance: Williamsburg, 1736

1. Farquhar, *Four Plays*, 13, 355, 402.
2. The "Life and Character" was prefixed to the 1718 edition of Farquhar's *The Stage Coach*, printed in London by S. Curll and R. Franklin (*Three Centuries of English Drama* [W&M micro]). Only the first two lines of the song were printed in *The Beaux' Stratagem* in Farquhar's works until the 1721 edition of the play.
3. *BU*, 855. The tune originally specified was the old air, "Sir Simon the King."
4. Farquhar, *Four Plays*, 354.
5. *VG*, September 10, 1736.
6. *LS*, pt. III, II, season of 1744–45; pt. IV, I, seasons of 1747–48 and 1748–49; Seilhamer, *History*, I, 41. Lewis Hallam, Sr., (1714–56), from the New Wells Theatre, Goodman's Fields, was accompanied by his actress wife and three of their four children. The company performed in the coastal colonies from 1752 until 1755, when it went to Jamaica, where Hallam died. His widow married David Douglass (ca. 1720–89); they brought the reorganized company, of which Douglass was the manager, back to the mainland in 1758 (Nagler, *Source Book*, 509, 511, 516).
7. *VG*, June 12, 1752.
8. *New York Mercury*, March 4, 1754.

[2]
THE SERENADE
(The Merchant of Venice)

Interpolated song; Shakespeare, *Variorum*, VII, *Merchant of Venice*, 96; "Words from an Ode in *The Spectator* by Sir Richard Steele." [*BU*, II, 670]

"Sung by Mr. Mattocks in *The Merchant of Venice*," S. sh. fol. (London: ca. 1770); bass given. [BM]

First performance of song: London, Drury Lane, 1741
First American performance: Williamsburg, 1752

1. *VG*, August 28, 1752; *VG*(PD), May 26, 1768.
2. Appleton, *Macklin*, 44, 48–50, 54, 73; Spencer, *Five Restoration Adaptations*, 29.
3. Cudworth, "Two Georgian Classics: Arne and Stevens," *ML*, XLV, 148; Cudworth, "Song and Part Song Settings," *Shakespeare in Music*, ed. Hartnoll, 61; *BU*, I, 41, 45; *BU*, II, 670; "The Serenade" retained its popularity, being set to new music as late as 1872 for an American performance of *The Merchant of Venice* (*Variorum*, 465).
4. *Variorum*, 96; Cudworth, "Song and Part Song Settings," *Shakespeare in Music*, ed. Hartnoll, 67; *BU*, II, 670; March 27, 1770, Covent Garden, "Mattocks—Lorenzo with Songs" (*LS*, pt. IV, III, 1465).
5. *LS*, pt. IV, II, index and seasons of 1757–58 and 1764–65; Clark, *Irish Stage*, 348; Odell, *New York Stage*, I, 125.

[3]
JESSICA'S SONG
(The Merchant of Venice)

Interpolated song; Shakespeare, *Variorum*, VII, *Merchant of Venice*, 93

S. sh. fol. (London: 1770); bass given. [BM]

First performance of song: London, Drury Lane, 1746
First American performance: Williamsburg, 1752

1. *LDA*, January 1, 1750; published by John Walsh; *BU*, I, 80, "Baildon," ca. 1750. Baildon was among the composers represented in *Love in a Village*.
2. *LDA*, March 4, 1746, Drury Lane.
3. Nagler, *Source Book*, 516; *LS*, pt. IV, II, 1088, Covent Garden, December 12, 1764; Willis, *Charleston Stage*, 49, 64. Miss Wainwright and Nancy Hallam, with Maria Storer and Stephen Woolls, sang at another benefit concert for Valton during the American Company's final colonial season in Charleston, February 15, 1774 (Willis, *Charleston Stage*, 64–65).

During the Revolution Miss Wainwright acted with the American Company in Jamaica, where she remained and married Isaac Morales, an actor and linguist (Wright, *Revels*, 50, 216).

4. Both Mrs. Parker and her husband, Charles (Rankin, *Theatre in Colonial America*, 141), had singing roles in the Virginia-New American Company.

[4]

COME HERE, FELLOW SERVANT

(High Life below Stairs)

London: J. Newbery, 1759. [W&M micro]	"Set by Mr. Battershill [*sic*] . . ." *London Magazine*, January, 1760; bass given. [HL]

First performance: London, Drury Lane, 1759
First known American performance: Philadelphia, 1767

1. Perhaps either "Marshall Lane's Minuet" or "Marshall Keith's Minuet," both of which are found in the manuscript music books of Robert Bolling (1738–75) and his son, Linnaeus (1773–1840), of Chellowe in Buckingham County, Virginia (Hubard Papers, vol. XXI, no. 360, Southern Historical Collection, University of North Carolina Library). Attention was called to the music books in this collection by Richard Beale Davis, *Intellectual Life in Jefferson's Virginia*, 321, who noted the presence in the music books of a minuet by "Mr. Pelham, Organist of the Church at Williamsburg." This is Pelham's only identified composition to date. Peter Pelham (b. London 1721, d. Virginia 1805) was a music teacher and organist in Williamsburg from 1755 to 1800. Pelham's minuet has been realized for Colonial Williamsburg Palace Concerts by Mr. James Darling, the present successor to Pelham as organist at Bruton Parish Church in Williamsburg.

2. Garrick, *Letters*, no. 188, p. 263 and no. 997, p. 1086.

3. Battishill, a church organist, at one time served as deputy to William Boyce, organist to the Chapel Royal. Brown and Stratton, "Battishill," *BMB*, 35; *Grove III*, 245–46; quoted in Cudworth, "Song and Part-Song Settings," *Shakespeare in Music*, ed. Hartnoll, 67.

4. Kitty Clive (b. Catherine Raftor, 1711, d. 1785) married George Clive, a lawyer, in 1732. Her acting career extended from 1728 to 1769 ("Catherine Clive," *DNB*); *Pennsylvania Gazette*, January 22, 1767, quoted in Pollock, *Philadelphia Theatre*, 21; *VG*(R), September 22, 1768; Odell, *New York Stage*, I, 141, 167; Margaret Cheer joined the American Company in 1764 after her arrival from London (ibid., 116). She remarried and, as Mrs. Long, kept a tavern in Jamaica, where she died in 1800 (Wright, *Revels*, 150).

5. Clark, *Irish Stage*, 375; Sheldon, *Thomas Sheridan*, 385; *Pennsylvania Packet*, December 14, 1772 [IEAHC micro].

6. Wright, *Revels*, 51–52, 345; Pollock, *Philadelphia Theatre*, 24; Seilhamer, *History*, I, 199.

7. *VG*(PD), May 26, 1768.

[5]

MY HEART WAS SO FREE

(The Beggar's Opera)

Moore, *Twelve Famous Plays*, 577–649; song text 591 (Act I, air 15)	Adaptation of melody in *PPM*, IV, 338; melody only. [CW]

First performance: London, Lincoln's Inn Fields, 1728
First known American performance: New York, 1750

COME, FAIR ONE, BE KIND

(The Recruiting Officer)

Farquhar, *Four Plays*, 243–352; song text, 283 (Act I, scene 1)	Same as above; "Sung by Mr. Wilks in The Recruiting Officer"

First performance: London, Drury Lane, 1706
First known American performance: New York, 1732

1. Playbill, CW; Rankin, *Theatre in Colonial America*, 141.

2. The "others" probably were musicians in or added to the company, to whom Pelham delegated some of the tasks. Pelham's assistant may have been the Italian-born instrumentalist and composer John (Giovanni) Gualdo, who had been teaching in Virginia; he later was associated with singers from the theatre in the concerts he conducted in Philadelphia (*Landon Carter Diary*, ed. Greene, I, 336; Sonneck, *Concerts*, 70–72).

3. Odell, *New York Stage*, I, 86.

4. Pepusch (b. Berlin 1667, d. London 1752) was a violinist and harpsichordist, Doctor of Music (Oxford, 1713), member of the Royal Society, a music director and composer at the London theatres in the first part of the century; Spacks, *John Gay*, 158.

5. Irving, *John Gay*, 10, 28, 93. A schoolmate of Gay's, the dramatist and writer of miscellany, Aaron Hill, wrote *The Walking Statue*, a farce performed in the colonies. Both Gay and Hill wrote librettos for Handel: Hill wrote *Rinaldo* in 1711 and Gay, *Acis and Galatea*, in 1731. Gay's ballad "Newgate's Garland" was sung in a play, *Harlequin Sheppard*, in 1724 (ibid., 235), where it was set to the tune of "Packington's Pound"—which was also used in *The Beggar's Opera*. "Newgate's Garland" is in John Edmunds's *A Williamsburg Songbook*, p. 53. Gay's works were owned by Virginians and advertised for sale in the *Virginia Gazette*.

6. Among early copies of *The Beggar's Opera* noted in Virginia was that in the 1734 inventory of Robert Beverley of Spotsylvania County (Spotsylvania County Will Book A, 1722–49) [VSL]; Byrd, "Progress to the Mines," *London Diary*, eds. Wright and Tinling, 627. William Byrd II (1674–1744) inherited Westover plantation from his father, the first of the name. Educated in England, the younger Byrd served as a member and president of the Virginia Council. His several surviving diaries cover a portion of the period he spent in England on the colony's business, and record his attendances at the theatres.

7. *Poems on Several Occasions* (facsimile reprint), 28–31; attributed to Dawson by Harold L. Dean (*Papers of the Bibliographical Society of America*, XXXI (1937), 10–20).

8. Seilhamer, *History*, I, 31. The company had performed it on June 22, in Annapolis, where they advertised as "from Virginia." They had played in Fredericksburg on June 2.

9. Sonneck, *Early Opera*, 18.

10. *VG*(PD), June 14, 1770; ibid., November 9, 1770 and March 14, 1771.

[6]

SWEET IS THE BUDDING SPRING OF LOVE

(Flora, or Hob in the Well)

London: T. Wood, 1729. [W&M micro]	Melody only printed with play text, with the tune title: "'Twas on a sunshine Summer's Day"

First performance: London, Lincoln's Inn Fields, 1729
First known American performance: Charleston, 1735

1. Nagler, *Source Book*, 510; Willis, *Charleston Stage*, 15; Sonneck, *Early Opera*, 12. Hob was the name used for a rustic clown.

2. "Hob's Opera—(afterpiece [John Hippisley]) Being the Farce of *The Country Wake* alter'd after the manner of *The Beggar's Opera*." (*LS*, pt. II, II, 1026), Lincoln's Inn Fields, April 17, 1729; Thomas Doggett (d. 1721) was a noted comic actor, theatre manager, and author of *The Country Wake;* Hughes and Scouten, *Ten English Farces*, 126–29; Irving, *John Gay*, 261; Burney, *History of Music*, II, 1000.

3. "'Twas on a sunshine Summer's Day" is the tune specified in the play text in the 1729 edition of the play; it is not the same as that for "Upon a sunshine Summer's Day," printed in *Pills to Purge Melancholy* (1699–1714). The source of the tune to "Sweet is the budding Spring" has not been traced.

4. "Mrs. Hallam" was listed in Williamsburg playbills for June 20, 1770 (*The Clandestine Marriage*) and May 1, 1771 (*Love in a Village*); she married Hallam in Jamaica before the company returned to the mainland in 1758; after her death he married another actress, Miss Eliza Tuke (Pollock, *Philadelphia Theatre*, 445); Odell, *New York Stage*, I, 86, January 1, 1762, as Flora; *New York Mercury*, March 22, 1762, as Flora [IEAHC micro]; Seilhamer, *History*, I, 144.

5. Odell, *New York Stage*, I, 173, *VG*(Pi), August 17, 1775.

6. Rosenfeld, *Theatre of the London Fairs*, 42; *LS*, pt. IV, I, 100, March 29, and *LDA* of same date; John Singleton and Patrick Malone performed with the Hallams in their first colonial seasons. Malone played Shylock in *The Merchant of Venice* at the opening performance in Williamsburg. *New York Mercury*, February 25, 1754; *Maryland Gazette*, May 1, 1760 [IEAHC micro].

[7]

A SOLDIER AND A SAILOR

(Love for Love)

Moore, *Twelve Famous Plays*, 255–342; song text, 308	"Sung by Mr. Doggett at the Theatre," *A Collection of Eighteenth-Century Single Sheet Songs*, IV, 13; bass given; [*BU* date: 1696]. [FL]

First performance: London, Lincoln's Inn Fields, 1695
First known American performance: New York, 1750

A FOX MAY STEAL YOUR HENS, SIR

(The Beggar's Opera)

Moore, *Twelve Famous Plays*, 577–649; song text, 588 (Act I, scene 9, air 11)	(See above)

First performance: London, Lincoln's Inn Fields, 1728
First known American performance: New York, 1750

1. Lonsdale, *Dr. Charles Burney*, 10.

2. Simpson, *BBB*, 670.

3. *LS*, pt. IV, I, 402 (see the commentary on "Billy Pringle's Pig," no. 44); *ESB*, no. 1603, p. 254 and no. 2443, p. 302; Avery, *Congreve's Plays*, 165; Thorp, *Songs from the Restoration Theatre*, 115–16. The play was advertised in Philadelphia in 1767 and again in 1770 with assurances that while its "Beauties" were preserved, its "Luxuriances" were to be "cropped" and its "Blemishes expunged" (Pollock, *Philadelphia Theatre*, 92, 112; see also Avery, *Congreve's Plays*, 111–15).

4. Congreve, dramatist and comanager in 1705 of the New Theatre in the Haymarket, was complimented by Sir Richard Steele on the "gentle, free, and easie Faculty" that distinguished his songs and short poems (Congreve, *Letters and Documents*, 80; Steele, *Occasional Verse*, ed. Blanchard, 14). Eccles, master of the king's Band of Musick, published in 1710 a collection of nearly one hundred songs, including many he had written for forty-six plays (*Grove V;* Thorpe, *Songs from the Restoration Theatre*, 217). Doggett established an annual prize for a watermen's race that is still awarded. *LS*, pt. I, 445, and pt. II, I, cxxvi.

5. Byrd, *London Diary*, 522, 525.

6. Avery, *Congreve's Plays*, 30; Byrd, *London Diary*, 94, and *LS*, pt. II, I, 487. Byrd mentions meeting Congreve at the home of friends several times during the period.

7. *New York Mercury*, October 22, 1753; Avery, *Congreve's Plays*, 99; *New York Mercury*, March 8, 1762.

8. Byrd, *Writings*, ed. Bassett, 413–43; Spotsylvania County Will Book B, 1749–59 [VSL], 234, appraisal, October 1, 1754; 245, library inventory, February 5, 1755; Simpson, *BBB*, 670; *LC*, Jefferson Collection, *Catalogue*, ed. Sowerby, IV, 4591, p. 554. This catalogue of the Jefferson library acquired for the Library of Congress lists a number of books pertaining to music and the theatre.

[8]

O ALL YE POWERS ABOVE

(The Virgin Unmask'd)

London: J. Watts, 1735. [W&M micro]	Music printed with play; Air, "Ye Nymphs and Sylvan Gods," from Thomas D'Urfey's play, *Don Quixote* (1695). (London: J. Watts, 1735); melody only. [W&M micro]

First performance: London, Drury Lane, 1735
First known American performance: New York, 1751

1. Cross, *Henry Fielding*, III, 298. Fielding was leaseholder and manager of the New Theatre in the Haymarket when his early career of play-writing was ended by the theatre licensing act of 1737. He later became a famous novelist (author of *Tom Jones* and *Joseph Andrew*) and a justice of the peace for Westminster and Middlesex.

2. Chappell, *Popular Music*, 295–97; Simpson, *BBB*, 490–92. Parker was a ballad writer whose career extended from the reign of James I into the Protectorate. Thomas D'Urfey (1653–1723) was a playwright, prolific contributor to the song collection *Wit and Mirth, or Pills to Purge Melancholy*, and editor of its final six volumes (*PPM*, I, 1, 4). D'Urfey's version of the poem with Eccle's tune was reprinted under various titles including "The Bonny (or Merry) Milk-Maid(s)" and "The Milking Pail" in broadside ballads and song collections, including D'Urfey's *Pills to Purge Melancholy*.

3. Farquhar, *Four Plays*, 292. Captain Plume sings part of the third verse in Act III, scene 1.

4. The title of the designated tune for this song in *Beau in the Suds* was erroneously printed in the 1730 text (Gilliver edition with the music; W&M micro) as "Sweet Nelly, my Heart's Delight," which has another air instead of "Young Nellie," one of this tune's alternative titles (Simpson, *BBB*, 492).

5. The play was in the Murray-Kean repertoire, 1751–52 (*Maryland Gazette*, July 9, 1752) during their Virginia-Maryland tour; in the Hallam Company repertoire (Nagler, *Source Book*,

510, and *New York Mercury*, October 8, 1753); the American Company repertoire, including the Virginia-Maryland seasons of 1760–62 (Seilhamer, *History*, I, 115); and in the Virginia-New American Company repertoire, 1768–69 (Sonneck, *Early Opera*, 45).

6. *LS*, pt. III, II, 1107; Mrs. Harman (1730–73) was the granddaughter of Colley Cibber, the dramatist, and his wife Catherine Shore, and the daughter of Richard Charke, composer, singing actor, and "First Violin" at Drury Lane, who died in Jamaica.

[9]
OVER THE HILLS AND FAR AWAY
(The Recruiting Officer)

Farquhar, *Four Plays*, 243–352; song text, 274, 276, 281 (Act II, scene 3)	*PPM*, V, 316; melody only. Song text, "The Recruiting Officer; or, the Merry Volunteers; Being an Excellent new copy of Verses upon raising Recruits," printed without music on p. 319, specified to be sung to the tune of the preceding song, "Jockey's Lamentation" (p. 316). [CW]

First performance: London, Drury Lane, 1706
First known American performance: New York, 1732

1. Farquhar, "The Recruiting Officer," *Regents Restoration Drama Series*, ed. Shugrue, ix. The words in the refrain, "Over the Hills, &c," used for both "Jockey's Lamentation" and for "Hark! now the Drums," are found in a broadside ballad of earlier date ("The Elfin Knight," in Bronson, *The Traditional Tunes of the Child Ballads*, I, 9).

2. Simpson, *BBB*, 562 fn; "A Song Set by Mr. [Richard] Leveridge, Sung in a Comedy call'd The Recruiting Officer" [Act III, scene 1](*PPM*, IV, 338). See "My Heart was so free," no. 5.

3. Farquhar, *Four Plays*, 12.

4. Byrd, *London Diary*, eds. Wright and Tinling, 522.

5. *VG*, September 10, 1736; Seilhamer, History, I, 33; F[airfax] H[arrison], "The Theatre in Eighteenth-Century Virginia, Outside of Williamsburg," *Virginia Magazine of History and Biography*, XXXV (July, 1927), 295–96.

6. Washington, *Diaries*, ed. Fitzpatrick, II, 5, January 23, 1771. Washington's diary and ledger of personal expenses reveal the presence in Williamsburg of the colonial theatre company when other sources are lacking or silent.

7. Willis, *Charleston Stage*, 27, 37, 66; Grant, *Memoirs of an American Lady*, 293.

8. The role of Plume was originated by Robert Wilks (1670–1732), a noted actor; Odell, *New York Stage*, I, 169.

9. McAleer, *Ballads and Songs Loyal to the Hanoverian Succession, 1703–1761*, 34. It is interesting to note that on March 17, 1746 Mr. and Mrs. Lewis Hallam, who six years later were to take an acting company to Virginia, selected *The Recruiting Officer* for their benefit performance at the Hallam Theatre in Goodman's Fields (*LS*, pt. III, II, 1226); they had made their first appearance at that theatre the preceding winter (ibid., 1149).

10. Simpson, *BBB*, 561–63; Franklin, *Autobiographical Writings*, ed. Van Doren, 88. Ralph was associated with Henry Fielding in managing the New Theatre in the Haymarket and in editing their thrice-weekly journal, *The Champion*.

11. *ODNR*, p. 408; lines from "Jockey's Lamentation":

Jockey [later Tom] was a piper's son,
And fell in love when he was young;
But all the tunes that he could play
Was O'er the Hills and far away.

Tom was a familiar name for pipers.

[10]
'TIS TRUE, MY GOOD DEAR
(The Mock Doctor)

London: J. Watts, 1732. [W&M micro]	*Songs in the Farce call'd The Mock Doctor*. (London: Printed and sold at the Musick Shops, 1732), melody only. [BM photo]

First performance: London, Drury Lane, 1732
First known American performance: New York, 1750

1. Edgar V. Roberts, "Mr. Seedo's London Career and His Work with Henry Fielding," *Philological Quarterly*, XLV (January, 1966), 183; Pedicord, *Theatrical Public*, 148. The most popular was *The Virgin Unmask'd*; other Fielding comedies and farces seen on the colonial stage were *The Miser*, *Don Quixote in England*, and *Tom Thumb*; all had music.

2. Roberts, *Philological Quarterly*, XLV (1966), 179, 181, 189; Fielding, *The Author's Farce*, ed. Woods, 93 fn, 94. The Prussian ambassador in London, Caspar Wilhelm von Borcke, Seedo's patron, had sent two shipments of Seedo's music to King Frederick at Potsdam, where the composer held a post with the royal band from 1736 until his death in 1754.

3. *New York Mercury*, December 14, 1761. The farce was an adaptation of Molière's *Le Médicin malgré lui* of 1666. Gregory as the mock doctor was a satirical impersonation of a French physician then resident in London, often the object of ridicule (Cross, *Henry Fielding*, I, 130–1).

4. Seilhamer, *History*, I, 7, 102, 114 ff; Odell, *New York Stage*, I, 34, 40, 76; Nagler, *Source Book*, 510; Seilhamer, *History*, I, 258–59. Its disappearance from the repertoire after 1769 may have been due to the "indelicate coarse kind of language offensive in these days of modern refinement," as it was castigated in a criticism of a Charleston performance in 1786 (Willis, *Charleston Stage*, 117).

5. Cross, *Henry Fielding*, I, 131–32; Mrs. Morris played in other singing roles, and was billed with songs between the acts at her benefit in Annapolis in 1760 (*Maryland Gazette*, May 8, 1760); Mr. and Mrs. Owen Morris were shareholders with Douglass in the company in Jamaica that combined with the Hallams and came to the mainland colonies in 1758 (Wright, *Revels*, 27–28); Willis, *Charleston Stage*, 51.

[11]
LET'S HAVE A DANCE
(Macbeth)

Spencer, ed., *Five Restoration Adaptations of Shakespeare*, 65 (Act II, scene 5)	Attributed to Matthew Locke by William Boyce. *The Original Songs in Macbeth*. Revised and corrected by Dr. Boyce. (London: Longman and Broderip, ca. 1780); bass given. [CW]

First performance: ca. 1663; song probably introduced 1702

First American performance: Philadelphia, 1759

1. For a comprehensive discussion of the *Macbeth* music and the reasons for identifying Leveridge as the composer of the music printed in the Boyce score, see Roger Fiske, "The 'Macbeth' Music," *ML*, XLV (April, 1964), 114–25. See also Robert Moore, "Music to Macbeth," *MQ*, XLVII (January, 1961), 22–40, and Charles Cudworth, "Song and Part-Song Settings of Shakespeare's Lyrics, 1660–1960," *Shakespeare in Music*, ed. Hartnoll, 53, in which he calls Boyce's attribution of the music to Locke "a puzzle for posterity." Boyce's ascription of the music to Matthew Locke is believed to have been based on the statement of John Downes, the theatre prompter and historian, who named Locke as providing the vocal music for the Davenant alteration of the play in 1663 (Fiske, "The 'Macbeth' Music," *ML*, XLV, 117; Downes, *Roscius Anglicanus*, 33). Henry Purcell, whose name was not linked with printed editions of the music until late in the eighteenth century, was credited with the music not only in the American Company's notice but in Irish playbills as early as 1749 at Smock Alley in Dublin (Sheldon, *Thomas Sheridan*, 333). The colonial and Irish companies may have attached Purcell's name to the music in their bills for reasons of prestige. Fiske suggests the same attitude was to be found in regard to the use of Purcell's or Locke's names in connection with the printed scores (Fiske, 121). He also suggests other reasons for the omission of Leveridge's name as the composer of the music.

2. *RMA Chronicle No. 1*, ed. Tilmouth, 45; *LS*, pt. II, I, 397; ibid., pt. IV, I, 219.

3. Mrs. Hallam was Lady Macbeth; Hallam, Macbeth; Adam Hallam, Malcolm. *LDA*, April 14, 1738. Leveridge's songs were familiar to colonials in plays and ballad operas, and in such collections as *Pills to Purge Melancholy*, the *Musical Miscellany*, Bickham, *Musical Entertainer*, and Leveridge's own collections, *A New Book of Songs*, 1697, and *A Collection of Songs in Two Volumes*, 1727.

4. Shakespeare, *Variorum*, *Macbeth*, 376, 519; Dent, *Foundations of English Opera*, 128; Moore, *Purcell*, 52.

5. *Pennsylvania Gazette*, October 25, 1759; the Harmans had appeared with William Hallam's company at Bartholomew Fair in London in September, 1756; Fiske, "The 'Macbeth' Music," *ML*, XLV, 123. Although Boyce assigned "Let's have a dance" to Hecate, two extant manuscript theatre copies differ on this point. In one, two women witches are to sing it; in the other, it is divided among a soprano, an alto, and a tenor; Spencer, *Five Restoration Adaptations*, 65; Seilhamer, *History*, I, 346.

6. See "Ye Gods, Ye gave to me a Wife," no. 12.

[12]
YE GODS, YE GAVE TO ME A WIFE
(The Devil to Pay)

London: J. Watts, 1732. [W&M micro]	S. sh. fol. (London: 1732); bass given. [BM photo]

First performance (three-act version): London, Drury Lane, 1731

First known American performance: Charleston, 1736

1. Hughes and Scouten, *Ten English Farces*, 175, 177–78; Pedicord, *Theatrical Public*, 147–48, 198–99; Loewenberg, *Annals of Opera*, col. 166, August 17, 1731. The composer Seedo's patron, von Borcke, Prussian ambassador in London, made the German translation of *The Devil to Pay*, first performed in Berlin in 1743 (Roberts, "Mr. Seedo's London Career," *Philological Quarterly*, XLV (1966), 181, 189.

2. Odell, *New York Stage*, I, 38; *Maryland Gazette*, August 3, 1752; Nagler, *Source Book*, 510.

3. Charles Coffey was an Irish dramatist who came to London in 1729, falsely encouraged by the reception of his ballad opera, *The Beggar's Wedding*, first performed in Dublin. John Mottley (1692–1750), who had been unsuccessful in keeping or securing various minor government posts, was a playwright and hack writer (Hughes and Scouten, *Ten English Farces*, 173–74; "Coffey" and "Mottley," *DNB*, also *Thespian Dictionary*).

4. Fielding, *The Author's Farce*, 85, Appendix A.

5. "Seedo," *Grove V*; Roberts, "Mr. Seedo's London Career," *Philological Quarterly*, XLV, (1966), 181, 189. His name was also spelled Sidou, Sedow, or Sydow.

6. The part of the blind fiddler was taken in 1772–73 by David Benjamin Roberts, an actor-singer and violinist with the American Company (Seilhamer, *History*, I, 297, 312; Wright *Revels*, 54); see "Love's a sweet and soft Musician," no. 16.

[13]
THE EARLY HORN
(The Devil to Pay)

Interpolated song from *The Royal Chace* (London: T. Wood, 1736). Words of song by Edward Phillips. [W&M micro]	*Universal Harmony* (London, Printed for J. Newbery, 1745), 96, score. (Opening recitative omitted here). [CW]

First performance (three-act version): London, Drury Lane, 1731

First known American performance: Charleston, 1736

1. "With Early Horn," *BU*, 1086; the song, one of the most popular of the eighteenth-century hunting songs, was issued in single-sheet copies from ca. 1737 through 1770 (see also *LS*, index entries after pt. III, II, 731 under "Early Horn"); *LS*, pt. III, II, 731; "Beard" (ca. 1717–91), *Grove V*, also *Thespian Dictionary; Royal Chace* (London: T. Wood, 1736); *LS*, pt. III, I, 546, Covent Garden, January 23, 1736: "Royal Chace or Merlin's Cave (with *Jupiter and Europa*); Endymion (as Royal Chasseur), Beard." One of the pantomimes with music by Galliard was *Apollo and Daphne, or The Burgomaster Trick'd. Harlequin Skeleton, or The Burgomaster Trick'd* was given by the Virginia Company as an afterpiece to *The Orphan* in Williamsburg in 1768 *VG*(PD), April 14, 1768). *Harlequin Skeleton* was an alternative title for *Merlin's Cave*, used with *The Royal Chace*, The skeleton scene from it was incorporated in other harlequin productions. *The Musical Miscellany* included seventeen of Galliard's songs.

2. Pollock, *Philadelphia Theatre*, 87; Odell, *New York Stage*, I, 126; *Pennsylvania Packet*, January 11, 1773; *LS*, pt. III, I, 150; Deutsch, *Handel*, 382, 473.

3. Willis, *Charleston Stage*, 74. It was the afterpiece to *Douglas*, advertised in 1774 as "the last Play for these three Years," a considerable understatement: The players did not return to Charleston until after the Revolution.

[14]

SABINA WITH AN ANGEL'S FACE

(The Careless Husband)

London: William Davis, 1705. [W&M micro]	"Sung by Mr. Leveridge Sett by Mr. Daniell Purcell." S. sh. fol. (London, 1707); bass given. [Birmingham, Eng., Public Library photo]

First performance: London, Drury Lane, 1704
First known American performance: New York, 1753

1. The play is considered important in the development of sentimental comedy. As a "genteel comedy," it was critically acclaimed throughout the century by Steele, Pope, Smollett, Horace Walpole, and others, with Fielding and Goldsmith the most notable dissenters (Barker, *Mr. Cibber of Drury Lane*, 47, 52–53); among the plays performed in the colonial repertoire that had musical entertainments mentioned in the play texts were Lillo's *George Barnwell*, Steele's *The Funeral*, and Cibber's *She Wou'd and She Wou'd Not* and *Love Makes a Man*.

2. Ibid., 176. Cibber often sang in company, unabashed even in the presence of Handel. The quality of his singing may be surmised from Aaron Hill's comparison of his speaking voice to that of a desperate pig (ibid., 33).

3. *LS*, pt. II, I, lxii and lxvii. Leveridge's singing career was long enough to permit him to sing for both Henry Purcell and Handel. *R.M.A. Research Chronicle*, I, 99, from *The Weekly Journal*, June 29, 1717: "A Punni-Musical Epistle to Mr. Daniel P[urcell] or a Letter in his own Way," signed "Signior Allegro" (mainly outrageous puns on musical terms). Purcell was called the "Pun-master General" by Sir Richard Steele.

4. *LS*, pt. II, I, entries for *The Careless Husband*, December 7, 1704 ff.; *New York Mercury*, December 3, 1753; Nagler, *Source Book*, 510.

5. Byrd, *Another Secret Diary*, ed. Woodfin, 202. (There is a variation in the last two lines: "When the Fellows all forsake her / Let her gnaw the Sheets and die.") Byrd, *London Diary*, eds. Wright and Tinling, 82–83, 114, 116, 158, 291, 338; ibid., 67, 96, 188, 253; *LS*, pt. II, II, 479, Lincoln's Inn Fields, January 18, 1718; 488, March 22, 1718; 511, October 27, 1718; 535, April 8, 1719.

[15]

INDIANA'S SONG

(The Conscious Lovers)

Taylor, ed., *Eighteenth-Century Comedy*, 101–90; song text, 105	"Sung in *The Conscious Lovers*," *The Musical Miscellany* (London: J. Watts, 1729), I, 104; melody only. [CW]

First performance: London, Drury Lane, 1722
First known American performance: New York, 1753

1. Giovanni Battista Bononcini: *Crispo*, London, January 31, 1722, and *Griselda*, London, March 22, 1722 (Loewenberg, *Annals of Opera*, vol. I, cols. 144, 139); Steele wanted incidental music in plays, but objected to Italian opera, where, according to Dryden's definition, the object was to please the hearing rather than gratify the understanding (Winton, *Captain Steel*, 70, 134; Westrup, *Purcell*, 128).

2. Hawkins, *History of Music*, II, 891.

3. The anonymous setting in *The Musical Miscellany* has been attributed to Galliard because of its style and proximity to others by him in the same collection. Steele and Galliard had both been members of the household of Prince George of Denmark, husband of Queen Anne, the composer as chamber musician and Steele as gentleman waiter; Steele, *Occasional Verse*, 26, 91, 86, 112; Loftis, *Steele at Drury Lane*, 183–85.

4. William Beverley, "A Diary of William Beverley of 'Blandfield' during a Visit to England, 1750," ed. R. Carter Beverley, *Virginia Magazine of History and Biography*, XXXVI (1928), 163; *LS*, pt. IV, I, 215.

5. Nagler, *Source Book*, 510. The play remained in the colonial repertoire and was still being given on the American stage after the Revolution (Pollock, *Philadelphia Theatre*, 168, 254, 389); Odell, *New York Stage*, I, 58–59, second and repeat performance by Hallam Company, New York, September 19, 1753.

6. Ibid., 61, in Hulett's advertisement to teach dancing, October 2, 1753. The Graniers (spelled Grenier in the advertisement), a family of French theatrical dancers, had performed at the Hallam's New Wells Theatre and at William Hallam's theatrical booth at Bartholomew Fair (*LS*, pt. III, I, cxv, cxxxvi, and March 14, 1743; Rosenfeld, *Theatre of the London Fairs*, 45, 49). Hulett also played small roles with the Hallam Company during the 1753–54 season. He remained in America and taught the violin as well as dancing. Mrs. Love's husband, the fifty-year-old Charles Love, one of the theatre instrumentalists who occasionally performed between the acts, gained notoriety in the colonial papers four years later by running away from his Virginia indenture with a bassoon belonging to Philip Ludwell Lee of Stratford, the Lee plantation in Westmoreland County. Love advertised to teach a variety of instruments in the same issue of the *New York Mercury* (July 2, 1753) in which Lewis Hallam's appeal for support in securing his promised theatre license was printed; *Maryland Gazette*, September 29, 1757.

[16]

LOVE'S A SWEET AND SOFT MUSICIAN

(The Musical Lady)

The Dramatick Works, vol. IV (London: T. Becket, 1777). [W&M micro]	"A Favourite Song sung by Miss Pope in *The Musical Lady*." S. sh. fol. (London: ca. 1775); bass given. [BM]

First performance: London, Drury Lane, 1762
First American performance: New York, 1769

1. *VG*(PD), October 17, 1771. A second, or possibly postponed performance of the same bill was advertised on October 24 for the next Saturday.

2. George Colman, whose son was also a well-known playwright, succeeded John Beard as manager at Covent Garden while Mr. and Mrs. George Mattocks and Charles Dibdin, the composer, were on the theatre's roster. He later took over the Haymarket Theatre from Samuel Foote. Colman's plays that were on the colonial stage (in addition to *The Musical Lady*, *The Jealous Wife*, and *The Clandestine Marriage*) were *Polly Honeycomb*, *The Deuce is in Him*, and *The English Merchant* ("George Colman the Elder," *Thespian Dictionary*; Page, *George Colman the Elder*, 74; Garrick, *Letters*, no. 261, p. 332 and no. 280, p. 348); *VG*(PD), December 9, 1771.

3. The arrival of Sophy's recently purchased armonica is announced by her maid, who explains it is the "Sett of Musical Glasses." "Armonica" was the name Benjamin Franklin gave the instrument that he had developed from the musical glasses

about a year before the first performance of the play (Franklin, *Autobiographical Writings*, ed. Van Doren, pp. 131–34). Its popularity was widespread; George Washington bought tickets to a performance on the armonica in Williamsburg in 1765 (Ford, *Washington and the Theatre*, 19). The play text for the concert rehearsal scene specifies "musicians, music stands, and everything prepared for a concert."

4. Byrom (1692–1763), a poet and the inventor of a shorthand system, was the author of the Christmas hymn "Christians, awake." His much quoted verses were later set as a glee by Peter Hellendaal in 1780. Deutsch, *Handel*, 178–180; Crane, *A Collection of English Poems*, 553–54. Garrick used the line again in 1766 in the pseudo-operatic epilogue to his and Colman's *Clandestine Marriage*, a play also given in Williamsburg (Moore, *Twelve Famous Plays*, 726; playbill, CW).

5. "Fonte Amiche" is a song in Handel's *Tolomeo, Re di Egitto* (1728).

6. Garrick, *Letters*, no. 268, p. 339. According to theatre custom Miss Pope had a music master, but at least one critic thought her singing left much to be desired (*LS*, pt. IV, III, 1447; ibid., 1297). Isabella was left with an aunt, Mrs. Mary Ann Barrington, "an actress of merit," and made her debut the same year (1752) at Covent Garden at the age of six in *Richard III* ("Isabella Mattocks," *Thespian Dictionary*). Nancy Hallam, the niece of Lewis Hallam, Sr., had appeared briefly with the American Company in children's roles in Philadelphia in 1759; she did not reappear in the colonies until the 1765–66 season (Wright, *Revels*, 38; Pollock, *Philadelphia Theatre*, 77). The name was spelled variously in theatre bills: Rozen, Rossini, etc. Roberts was with the American Company in the colonies from 1767 until 1774; he played the blind fiddler in *The Devil to Pay* and had a singing role in *Midas* (Seilhamer, History, I, 360; Wright, *Revels*, 54, 298).

7. Odell, *New York Stage*, I, 149; Pollock, *Philadelphia Theatre*, 107.

8. "Musical Lady," *BU*, I, 719.

[17]
WATER PARTED FROM THE SEA
(Artaxerxes)

Score [CW]	Full score (London: Printed for J. Johnson 1762). [CW]

First performance: London, Covent Garden, 1762, "An English Opera"
Not performed in America until nineteenth century

1. Oxford awarded Arne the doctorate in 1759. Metastasio (1698–1782) was an Italian poet called the librettist to all Europe; "Metastasio," *Grove III*; Belden, *Samuel Foote*, 123.

2. Loewenberg, *Annals of Opera*, "Artaxerxes," 1762, col. 257.

3. Odell, *New York Stage*, I, 103. According to Sonneck (*Early Opera*, 34), "Water parted from the Sea" was sung at the end of a performance of *Damon and Phillida* in Philadelphia on June 5, 1766. The year is probably an error for 1769, when Pollock (*Philadelphia Theatre*, 107) records a performance of the play for the same month and day. There is no mention of it in his calendar of plays for the same date in 1766 (ibid., 84–85); Odell, *New York Stage*, I, 117.

4. Fithian, *Journal*, 30, 37, 51; Carter (1728–1804), educated in England and member of the Council of Virginia, had ordered his armonica from London in 1764 after Peter Pelham, the Williamsburg organist, described it to him. Pelham had heard Benjamin Franklin perform on it in New York (Robert Carter of Nomini Hall, to John Jordan, May 23, 1764, Mss Letterbook, 1764–68, CW; see also *Oxford Companion to Music*, Scholes, ed., [1955] p. 442 and plate 91). At Nomini Hall, Carter also had a harpsichord, piano, guitar, violin, and German flutes.

5. Fithian, *Journal*, 71. This song, "Infancy" or "In Infancy," was published in several British periodicals with Virginia subscribers, including the *London Magazine* and the *Universal Magazine*, between 1762 and 1764 (*BU*, I, 42, 542), and was one of nineteen tunes on a barrel organ that was advertised for sale in Pennsylvania in 1771 (*Pennsylvania Packet*, October 28, 1771). Later the tune was adapted to the nursery song "The Queen of Hearts" (Arne, "Artaxerxes," *BU*, I, 42).

6. Hubard Papers, vol. XXI, no. 360, Southern Historical Collection, University of North Carolina Library. Ferdinando Tenducci, an Italian opera singer, the Arbaces in the original performance, was much admired for his singing of the aria (*LS*, pt. IV, II, 915, Covent Garden, February 2, 1762; "Tenducci," *Grove III*).

[18]
CASTALIO'S COMPLAINT
(The Orphan)

Bell, *British Theatre*, IX; song text, 86 [W&M]	*A Collection of Eighteenth-Century Single-Sheet Songs*, IV, 187; figured bass given; (*BU* date: ca. 1730). [FL]

First performance: London, Dorset Garden, 1680
First known American performance: Charleston, 1735

1. Odell, *New York Stage*, I, 34; Otway's emphasis on the human emotions in this play and in his *Venice Preserv'd* was an innovation in Restoration tragedy (Nettleton, *English Drama*, 100–101); *Venice Preserv'd* was also in the colonial repertoire.

2. Wood, *Personal Recollections of the Stage*, 27; after the Revolution Henry, "a good musical performer," assisted the orchestra as a violinist whenever his duties as actor-manager permitted (ibid., 25; Pollock, *Philadelphia Theatre*, 23); Virginia Company of Comedians, playbill for Friday, April 15, 1768, CW; Pollock, *Philadelphia Theatre*, 101; Willis, *Charleston Stage*, 51.

3. Ibid., 11; Seilhamer, *History*, I, 2.

4. *VG*, May 24, 1751; Byrd, *Writings*, ed. Bassett, 413–43; LC, Jefferson Collection, *Catalogue*, ed. Sowerby, IV, 538, no. 4544.

5. Forcer composed the setting for the song in *The Orphan* in 1680, and it was published the following year in *Choice Ayres* (Thorp, *Songs from the Restoration Theatre*, 38–39) and reprinted in various editions of *PPM* through 1719 (*ESB*, no. 591, p. 196); Thorp, *Songs from the Restoration Theatre*, 99. Boyce (Doctor of Music, Cambridge, 1749) was an organist, composer of church and theatre music, and collector and editor of a great three-volume work of cathedral music.

[19]
THE LIFE OF A BEAU
(The Miser)

Dublin, G. W. Rich, 1733. [W&M micro] Interpolated song text by James Miller, from the farce, *The Coffee House.*	"Set by Mr. Carey, The Words by Mr. J. Miller, sung by Mrs. Clive," Bickham, *The Musical Entertainer*, II, 50; bass given. [CW]

First performance of play: London, Drury Lane, 1733
First performance of interpolated song, 1739
First known American performance: Philadelphia, 1767

1. CW playbill collection; *The Brave Irishman* was the afterpiece (see "Ballynamony," no. 20); Cross, *Henry Fielding*, 144–46.

2. *LS*, pt. III, II, 787; ibid., 698. The Rev. James Miller (1706–44) was a playwright and author of a libretto for Handel, *Joseph and His Brethren.*

3. Ibid., pt. IV, I and II, September, 1739 through January 18, 1765, passim; ibid., I, 103, March 13, 1749: alterations made in Fielding's *The Intriguing Chambermaid* enabled her to sing the song as Lettice, a part written for her by the author, who held her in the highest regard (Cross, *Henry Fielding*, 145).

4. Burney, *History*, II, 1000; Deutsch, *Handel*, 559, 427, 470.

5. *LS*, pt. III, II, 1122; Burney, *History*, II, 999.

6. A silver ticket was a permanent token that honored the holder with a free seat in the theatre at any time (Sheldon, *Thomas Sheridan*, 115); possibly *Catone in Utica*, given the preceding fall at the King's Theatre (Deutsch, *Handel*, 296).

7. Willis, *Charleston Stage*, 51; *LS*, pt. IV, II, 748.

[20]
BALLYNAMONY
(The Brave Irishman)

Hughes and Scouten, *Ten English Farces*, 227–37; song text, 236	"Balin a mone, sung by Mr. Barington in *The Double Disappointment*," s. sh. fol. (London: ca. 1750); bass given. [University of Glasgow Library photo]

First London performance: New Wells, Goodman's Fields, 1746
First known American performance: New York, 1765

1. Seilhamer, *History*, I, 166. Mendez (d. 1758) was a stockbroker and playwright; his little opera, *The Chaplet*, with music by Boyce, also was given on the colonial stage.

2. Oliver Goldsmith designated the tune "Baleinamony" for the song "Ye Brave Irish Lads" that he wrote as an epilogue for *She Stoops to Conquer* (Goldsmith, *Collected Works*, IV, 394). John Barrington (1715–73), popular Irish actor-singer, was the second husband of Mary Ann Hale, an actress and a Hallam aunt. The Lewis Hallams left their daughter Isabella with her when they went to Virginia.

3. *LS*, pt. III, II, 1215.

4. For problems concerning the performance and edition dates see Hughes and Scouten, *Ten English Farces*, 222–25; see also Sheldon, *Thomas Sheridan*, 20–28, especially p. 26 for date of first version, 1740–41.

5. Seilhamer, *History*, I, 198; Clark, *Irish Stage*, 361; Seilhamer, *History*, I, 222; Odell, *New York Stage*, 135. Henry (1746–94) was said to be "inimitable in Irish parts" ("John Henry," *Dictionary of American Biography*).

6. CW playbill collection; Willis, *Charleston Stage*, 44–45; *The Brave Irishman* and *The Way to Keep Him* had been given in Charleston in 1766 at a benefit performance for Verling, with his brother Masons in attendance, during his first American season (ibid., 53–54).

7. Odell, *New York Stage*, I, 148.

[21]
FAREWELL, UNGRATEFUL TRAYTOR
(The Spanish Friar)

Bell, *British Theatre*. II [W&M]	"A Song, set by Mr. Pack," *PPM*, V, 334–35, melody only. [CW]

First performance: London, Dorset Garden, 1680
First known American performance: Charleston, 1735

1. The allusion is unidentified. Perhaps the reference is to Olympias, the mother of Alexander the Great. The song text is printed in the play.

2. *LS*, pt. I, 292; November 1, 1680.

3. Dryden wrote many song texts for his plays. *LS*, pt. I, 371, May 28, 1689; Murrie, *Restoration Court Stage*, 102fn, 199.

4. Thorp, *Songs from the Restoration Theatre*, 99–102; *ESB*, no. 974, p. 218; Simpson, *BBB*, 215–16. Pack's career, as well as his life, nearly came to an end when, as one of the "Portsmouth captains," he revolted against the policy of Irish recruitment for James II's army. He was broken, but reinstated and served at the battle of the Boyne, being promoted to colonel in 1689.

5. Odell, *New York Stage*, I, 63; Nagler, *Source Book*, 511, 513; Pollock, *Philadelphia Theatre*, 75; Odell, *New York Stage*, I, 58–59. Since the Miss Hallam of the casts played mature roles, it is possible that both Hallam's sister and his daughter were with the company for a brief period. If Miss Hallam were the sister, she may have been the youngest member of the family group that in 1733 acted in Canterbury in a company from both London theatres royal. Then, as "Miss Hallam, Junior," she played the child part of the Duke of York in *Richard III*, and Lewis Hallam on that occasion was billed as "Young Hallam." (Rosenfeld, *Strolling Players*, 59.)

6. The inventory of Carter's library included collections of plays as well as seventeen volumes of unidentified music. The Byrd library at Westover had two different editions of his plays, three volumes of his poems, and a folio edition of his *Works*. The unidentified *Tragedies and Operas* in one-volume octavo in the Byrd inventory may have been Dryden's *Comedies, Tragedies, and Operas*, published the year after his death, in 1701 (*British Authors Before 1800*, Kunitz and Haycraft, eds.; Byrd, *Writings*, Bassett, ed., 413–43). Henry Purcell, who had provided music for other of Dryden's plays, set another song for a revival of *The Spanish Friar*, "Whilst I with Grief," in 1695.

[22]
DIRGE
(Cymbeline)

"A song from Shakespeare's *Cymbeline* sung by Guiderius and Arviragus over Fidele, supposed to be dead," as titled in the *Gentleman's Magazine*, October, 1749 (Crane, ed., *Collection of English Poems*, 741), probably sung in Act V, scene 3, Garrick's adaptation (London: 1762), p. 60. [W&M micro]	Score in s. sh. fol. (London: ca. 1760). [BM photo]

First performance (Garrick version): London, Drury Lane, 1761
First known American performance: Philadelphia, 1767

1. Odell, *New York Stage*, I, 171; Seilhamer, *History*, I, 281, 289; *Maryland Gazette*, November 7, 1771.

2. Cudworth, "Song and Part-Song Settings," *Shakespeare in Music*, ed. Hartnoll, 61–62.

3. *New York Mercury*, December 28, 1767; Seilhamer, *History*, I, 155, 212.

4. *Pennsylvania Packet*, December 7, 1772; Odell, *New York Stage*, I, 171; letter printed in *Maryland Gazette*, September 6, 1770; Seilhamer, *History*, I, 281–89; Willis, *Charleston Stage*, 52; Pollock, *Philadelphia Theatre*, 22; "Letter written by Hudson Muse of Virginia . . .," *William and Mary Quarterly*, 1st ser., II (1894), 239–41.

5. Boucher, *Reminiscences*, 13, 66. Boucher (1737–1804) was a loyalist who returned to England at the time of the Revolution. As a boy in England he was almost persuaded to enter a theatrical career by James Dance, who under his stage name of Love became a prominent actor and wrote *The Witches*, an afterpiece performed in the colonies (Garrick, *Letters*, I, no. 322, p. 401).

[23]
AILEEN AROON
(Love a-la-Mode)

An inter-act song attributed to Carrol O'Daly, introduced into a New York performance of *Love a-la-Mode*, June 24, 1773 by Maria Storer. Play text: London, no publisher, 1784. [W&M micro]. Translation courtesy of Mr. R. J. Hayes, Director, National Library of Ireland

A Collection of Eighteenth-Century Single Sheet Songs, I, 64; bass given; (*BU* date: ca. 1740). [FL]

First performance of play: London, Drury Lane, 1759
First known performance of song in play in America: New York 1773

1. Odell, *New York Stage*, I, 167–68. Sir Callaghan explains to Charlotte that she must not expect fine singing from him, "for we Irishmen are not cut out for it like the Italians."

2. Ibid.; also p. 135 (May 13, 1768 in New York, singing between the acts, *Venice Preserv'd* and *Love a-la-Mode*); playbill for May 22, 1771, CW.

3. *LS*, pt. III, II, 974 ff.; ibid., pt. IV, I, 39 ff; Deutsch, *Handel*, 556–72; *LDA*, July 29, 1748; *LS* pt. IV, I and II, passim; Wright, *Revels*, 52; Sonneck, *Early Opera*, 37.

4. O'Sullivan, *Carolan*, I, 17, 18. According to tradition, "Eibhlin-a-Ruin" figured in O'Daly's romantic elopement with Lady Kavanagh of Clonmullen Castle, County Wexford, Ireland; Monticello Music Collection, on deposit in Alderman Library, University of Virginia, Charlottesville; printed at the end of the song in the *European Magazine* is: "words supplied by the Rt. Honourable, the Secretary of State for Ireland [John Heely Hutchinson]" (*Music in the Huntington Library*, ed. Backus, 825); Cushing, "Robin Adair," *Children's Song Index*. Lady Caroline Keppel, daughter of the earl of Albemarle (an absentee governor of Virginia), wrote the words before her marriage in 1758 to Robert Adair.

5. *The Reprisal* by Tobias Smollett (1721–71) was in the colonial repertoire; in a Charleston playbill of 1774 Lt. O'Clabber was listed "with a Song." (Seilhamer, *History*, I, 334; Willis, *Charleston Stage*, 71); *Music in the Huntington Library*, 825.

6. Appleton, *Charles Macklin*, 14. Macklin's varied experiences as a strolling player had included writing and setting to popular airs the songs he sang at performances. Macklin (1699–1797) called this play his "favourite feather, the best in my cap" (Findlay, "Macklin's Legitimate Acting Version of *Love a-la-Mode*," *Philological Quarterly*, XLV, (October, 1966), 751, 754–57). In 1785 he sued a Dublin manager who infringed on his rights (Appleton, *Charles Macklin*, 117).

[24]
THE SERENADING SONG
(The Constant Couple)

Farquhar, *Four Plays*, 37–138; song text, 105 (Act IV, scene 3)

"Sung by Mr. Freeman," *PPM*, VI, 36; [CW] and s. sh. fol., (London: 1700); bass given. [CW]

First performance: London, Drury Lane, 1699
First known American performance: Norfolk, 1751

1. The play's subtitle refers to the Papal Jubilee at Rome in 1699, which attracted English tourists, and to which Beau Clincher, "the pert London apprentice," is always preparing to depart. (Congreve, *Letters and Documents*, 21, 22, n. 9.)

2. Purcell had been organist at Magdalene College, Oxford; Jefferson owned his *Psalms Set full for the Organ or Harpsichord* (London: Printed for J. Walsh and John Hare, 1715).

3. For Pate, see "She walks as she dreams," no. 42. Freeman was the composer of one of the tunes used in *The Beggar's Opera*. At four other places in the comedy the author arranged for Sir Harry to sing, but the "serenading song" is the only one printed in its entirety in the play.

4. *VG*, April 17, 1752. Landon Carter, attending the Assembly sessions in Williamsburg, had unwillingly accompanied two fellow burgesses to the theatre two days earlier and had nothing kind to say about the players (*Landon Carter Diary*, ed. Greene, I, 103). Kean played singing roles and was featured as an inter-act singer.

5. Seilhamer, *History*, I, 49, New York, October 1, 1753; Odell *New York Stage*, I, 59–60; playbill for Wednesday, May 10, 1768, CW; possibly the minuet occurs at the point where the text calls for "singing and dancing," with no other specification (Farquhar, *Four Plays*, 127).

[25]
DEAR PRETTY YOUTH
(The Tempest)

Interpolated song; text of play, in Spencer, ed., *Five Restoration Adaptations of Shakespeare*, 109–98. Song text, *Orpheus Britannicus*, 78

Orpheus Britannicus (London: Playford, 1698), 78; bass given. [CW]

First performance of "operatic" version: London, Dorset Garden, 1674; song probably introduced ca. 1695
First known American performance: Philadelphia, 1770

1. Shakespeare, *Complete Works*, 1298; Shakespeare, *Variorum, The Tempest*, 306, 308–15; Abbot, *A Virginia Chronology, 1585–1783*, 5; Jester and Hiden, eds. "Strachey," *Adventurers of Purse and Person*, 319–20; ibid., Letter to Lady Willoughby de Broke.

2. Spence, *Anecdotes*, 45; Downes, *Roscius Anglicanus*, 34. The size and disposition of the orchestra as described at the beginning of the play text (Shakespeare *Variorum*, 392) has been considered one of the landmarks in theatre music (Thorp, *Songs from the Restoration Theatre*, 4, and Moore, *Henry Purcell*, 186–87). Thomas Shadwell (1642–92) did an alteration that differed very little from the Dryden-Davenant version except for the provision of more music and spectacle (ibid. 179).

3. Dean, "Shakespeare and Opera," *Shakespeare in Music*, ed. Hartnoll, 105–106; Shakespeare, *Variorum*, *The Tempest*, 390; Spencer, *Five Restoration Adaptations*, 17–18, 112; Fiske, "Shakespeare in the Concert Hall," *Shakespeare in Music*, ed. Hartnoll, 223; Cudworth, "Song and Part-Song Settings of Shakespeare's Lyrics," ibid., 54.

4. Dean, "Shakespeare and Opera," ibid., 106; Moore, *Henry Purcell*, 195–96; Burney, *History*, II, 382; plays in the colonial repertoire for which Purcell had set the music were *Amphitryon*, *Theodosius*, *The Spanish Friar*, and *The Tempest* with its masque, *Neptune and Amphitrite*.

5. In *Deliciae Musicae, Being a Collection of the newest and best Songs Sung at Court and at the Publick Theatres* (1696) (*ESB*, no. 821, p. 209) and *Orpheus Britannicus*, the posthumous collection of Purcell's songs, published in 1698 and in new editions in 1706 and 1721. Purcell's music was written for the Shadwell alteration of the Dryden-Davenant adaptation (Dean, "Shakespeare and Opera," *Shakespeare in Music*, ed. Hartnoll, 105). For example, Drury Lane, December 26, 1739, "Dorinda, with song, Dear Pretty Youth, Mrs. Clive," and May 15, 1741, "Dear Pretty Youth, sung by Mrs. Clive" (*LS*, pt. III, II, 811, 917); Dublin, season 1756–57 (Sheldon, *Thomas Sheridan*, 467–68); Moore, *Henry Purcell*, 195–96; Spencer, *Five Restoration Adaptations*, 179–81.

6. Seilhamer, *History*, I, 270. A Charleston announcement as late as April 20, 1793, referred to the play as "written by Shakespeare, alter'd by Dryden," and to the music as "compos'd by that learned and excellent man, Dr. Purcell." The description of the scenery and mechanical effects for the opening scene of the storm shows great similarity to the description of the Shadwell performance over one hundred years before. (Willis, *Charleston Stage*, 171; Shakespeare, *Variorum*, *The Tempest*, 392). The masque, which had been added during the Restoration as a balance to the spectacular storm that opened the play, according to the announcement was "to terminate the whole . . . in a view of a calm'd Sea, in which Neptune and Amphitrite appear in a Shell Chariot drawn by Sea Horses" (Willis, *Charleston Stage*, 171–72). Composers of music for the masque included Pelham Humphrey (1674), Henry Purcell (1695), and Thomas Arne (about 1746).

7. Seilhamer, *History*, I, 272; May 10, 1773, New York (Odell, *New York Stage*, I, 163); Seilhamer, *History*, II, 181 (New York, May 31, 1786); during the Constitutional Convention in Philadelphia *The Tempest* was given on July 14, 1787 in the traditional (Dryden-Davenant) version; George Washington was present at the performance (Ford, *Washington and the Theatre*, 33).

8. *Maryland Gazette*, November 7, 1771; a performance may also have been given in Fredericksburg when the company played there in May 1771. Appearances of the players often coincided with the race meetings at the fairs, so it may be significant that one of the racing entries at the October fair in 1774 at Fredericksburg was called Ariel. (Harrower, *Journal*, 141, 189.)

[26]

WHER' DID YOU BORROW THAT LAST SIGH?

(The Lost Lady)

Dodsley, *Select Collection of Old English Plays*, XII, 537–627; song text, 599	Autograph score, BM Add. Mss. 31432; bass given

First performance: London, ca. 1637

1. Lefkowitz, *William Lawes*, 16. Lawes, one of the king's musicians for lutes and voices, and his brother, Henry, set music to the biblical paraphrases written by George Sandys, secretary of the Virginia Company. (Sandys lived in the colony between 1621 and 1628). A number of these were published by Henry Lawes in *Choice Psalms* in 1648 (ibid., 17, 18, 236).

2. Bald, "Sir William Berkeley's *The Lost Lady*," *The Library*, series IV, vol. 7 (1937), 395; Abbot, *A Virginia Chronology*, 17; Lefkowitz, *William Lawes*, 20–21.

3. Ibid., 195.

4. Bald, "Sir William Berkeley's *The Lost Lady*," 395; *LS*, pt. I, 23, 152, January 19 and 28, 1661. Berkeley's second and now lost play *Cornelia* may have been written in Virginia during the interregnum while he was living at his Green Spring plantation near Jamestown. The play was given in London (*LS*, pt. I, 38) before his return to Virginia in 1662. Berkeley, who was removed from office in 1677 after Bacon's Rebellion, returned to England and died there.

[27]

THERE'S NOT A SWAIN

(Damon and Phillida)

London: J. Watts, 1729. [W&M micro]	Play text, "with Music prefix'd"; melody only. Bass adapted from "There's not a Swain," *The Gentleman's Journal*, April 1694, pp. 101–3. [HL]

First performance: London, Drury Lane, 1729
First known American performance: New York, 1751

1. Cibber selected the names of his characters from classical or pseudo-classical sources. Cymon, spelled Cimon in the first edition and early casts of the play, was the name of a distinguished Athenian, son of Miltiades, the victor at Marathon.

2. *LS*, pt. II, II, 853, February 2, 1726; this was one of the terms of respect frequently used over the next century in connection with Purcell's name (see, for example, *RMA Research Chronicle, No. 2*, 17, and Willis, *Charleston Stage*, 171); Zimmerman, *Henry Purcell: Analytical Catalogue*, 587; *LS*, pt. I, 408; Zimmerman, *Henry Purcell: Life and Times*, 234; *LS*, pt. I, 429; *ESB*, 88, no. 3251, p. 348; Zimmerman, *Life and Times*, ibid.; "A song, the notes by Mr. Henry Purcell, the words fitted to the tune by N. [*sic*] Henley, Esq.," *Gentleman's Journal*, April, 1694, 101–3 [HL photocopy]. Ballad operas performed in the colonies in which Purcell's tunes were used included *The Beggar's Opera*, *Damon and Phillida*, *The Virgin Unmask'd*, *The Mock Doctor*, *Don Quixote in England*, *The Devil to Pay*, and *Beau in the Suds*. The *Journal* was one of the periodicals in the inventory of the Byrd library at Westover.

3. See "The Romp's Song"; Sonneck, *Catalogue* 165; *BU*, "H. Carey," 165, Air 7, "A Swain long tortured with disdain,"

ca. 1720–25; Ashley, *Colley Cibber*, 76–78. Cibber's wife, Catherine Shore, a singing actress and member of the famous family of trumpeters, had been Purcell's pupil in voice and harpsichord.

4. *VG*, June 12, 1752, announcing the imminent arrival of "Mr. Hallam from the New Theatre in Goodman's Fields, London, with a select Company of Comedians"; Nagler, *Source Book*, 510; Seilhamer, *History*, I, 236, April 8, 1768, by the Virginia Company; November 23, 1771, by the American Company (Sonneck, *Early Opera*, 46).

5. Seilhamer, *History*, I, 46. Presumably the Miller in the colonies was the actor who appeared with the Hallam Company at Goodman's Fields during the 1744–45 season (*LS*, pt. III, II, 1117). The first edition of *Damon and Phillida* lists Cibber's son-in-law, Richard Charke, father of the American Company's Catherine Maria Harman, as Damon, and Catherine Raftor (later Mrs. Clive) as Phillida, a part she played for the rest of her career. A picture of her in the role is reproduced in *LS* pt. IV, I, following p. 176, from one in the Folger Library.

6. Sonneck, *Early Opera*, 46.

[28]

WHEN DAMON LANGUISH'D

(The Gamester)

Booth, ed. *Eighteenth-Century Tragedy*, 155–225; song text, 196 (Act III)	"Song in The Gamester, set by Mr. Oswald," *Gentleman's Magazine*, XXV, (February, 1755), 83; bass given. [CW]

First performance: London, Drury Lane, 1753
First known American performance: New York, 1754

1. Willis, *Charleston Stage*, 52.

2. Seilhamer, *History*, I, 57, and Odell, *New York Stage*, I, 66, February 4, 1754; *LS*, pt. IV, I, 350, February 7, 1753; *VG*(PD), May 19, 1768; no cast given. The play probably was given in earlier and later seasons in Williamsburg.

3. "Edward Moore," *DNB*; Garrick, *Letters*, no. 120, p. 186–87; Rosenfeld, *Strolling Players*, 195.

4. The Clarksons were minor players with the Hallam Company from 1753 to 1755; a Clarkson was listed in the cast with Lewis Hallam at the Haymarket, August 26, 1750. Odell, *New York Stage*, I, 66, February 4, 1754, and 163, May 10, 1773; Willis, *Charleston Stage*, 53, March 4, 1766; Pollock, *Philadelphia Theatre*, 95, April 2, 1767.

5. Oswald played the cello in concerts and at Drury Lane, where he was an associate of Burney, with whom he later engaged in music publishing (*LDA*, August 31, 1746, July 26, 1749; *LS*, pt. III, II, December 1 and 3, 1743, Drury Lane; Lonsdale, *Dr. Charles Burney*, 25, 28–32). Oswald was under the patronage of the Prince and Princess of Wales; their son, who became George III and who probably was his pupil, appointed Oswald his chamber musician in 1761. Johnson, *Scots Musical Museum*, 407; letter of Franklin, June 2, 1765, to Lord Kames [Henry Home, 1696–1782] in which Franklin wrote that he wished Kames, in his *Elements of Criticism*, "had examined more fully the subject of Music." Franklin referred to the beauties and simplicities of the Scottish tunes, especially as played by Oswald on his cello (Franklin, *Papers*, ed. Labaree, XII, 162–64).

[29]

IF THE SWAIN WE SIGH FOR

(Midas)

London: T. Lowndes, 6th ed., 1771. [CW]	"Sung by Miss Hallam in the Character of Nysa" *Midas, a Comic Opera*, for Harpsichord, Voice, German Flute, or Guitar. Sung by Miss Hallam, Miss Miller, Miss Poitier, Mr. Beard, Mr. Mattocks, and Mr. Fawcett. (London: Printed for J. Walsh [1764]). [CW]

First performance: Dublin, 1762
First American performance: Philadelphia, 1769

1. Loewenberg, *Annals of Opera*, "Midas," 1762, col. 256; *LS*, pt. IV, II, 1151; *Midas* was revised from three acts to two, February 5, 1766, Covent Garden; *VG*(PD), August 29, 1771.

2. Willis, *Charleston Stage*, 68; Charleston playbill for April 25, 1774, lists "Fabulous Deities" in the cast; in the 1771 edition of the play (London: T. Lowndes), it is "The Heathen Deities" that are discovered at the curtain's rise; in mythology Silenus was the tutor of Bacchus; Nysa's name perhaps was derived from Nysas, the birthplace of Bacchus; Daphne was the river nymph pursued by Apollo and changed into a bay tree.

3. *LS*, pt. IV, II, 1106, April 8, 1765.

4. Hubard Papers, vol. 21, no. 20, Southern Historical Collection, University of North Carolina, Chapel Hill. Bolling had two music books bound at the *Virginia Gazette* in Williamsburg in 1764 (Royle Daybook, August 11, 1764); Bolling studied law with Benjamin Waller in Williamsburg after attending grammar school in England with several other Virginia boys (Baine, *Robert Munford*, 6–7); Thomas Jefferson Collection of Music at Alderman Library, University of Virginia, Charlottesville.

[30]

ALL AROUND THE MAYPOLE

(Midas)

T. Lowndes 1771. [CW]	"Sung by Mr. Fawcett in the Character of Damaetas." (See "If the Swain we sigh for," no. 29). [CW]

First performance: Dublin, 1762
First American performance: Philadelphia, 1769

1. "Kane O'Hara," *Thespian Dictionary*; a burletta is a form of musical comedy bridging the gap between ballad opera and comic opera. It came from Italy through France, but the English burletta was really created by O'Hara's *Midas* ("Burletta," *Grove III*); among airs selected were some from *PPM* (1699–1720), but others were scarcely "old." Music was taken from Carey's *The Honest Yorkshireman* (1735), Handel's *Judas Maccabeus* (1747), and Boyce's *The Chaplet* (1749); Loewenberg, *Annals of Opera*, "Midas," 1762, col. 256; Deutsch, *Handel*, 808.

2. *Oxford Companion to English Literature*, 3rd. ed., 540–41; the chanter is the melody pipe (as opposed to the drones) of

the bagpipe. John Sutherland was paid five shillings a night "for playing the bagpipes in *Midas*" (*LS*, pt. IV, I, cxxix; *LS*, pt. IV, II, 1196 [Covent Garden Account Books, 1766–68]).

3. Damaetus was a herdsman in Theocritus and Vergil; in pastoral poetry the name was identified with a rustic, but in Sir Philip Sidney's *Arcadia* it was the name of a foolish country clown; thereafter it was proverbial for folly; the tune was used in later years for the children's song, "The little woman and the pedlar" (*Music Hour, Third Book*, 120); a Scottish version of these verses set to another tune is in Johnson, *Scots Musical Museum*, no. 491, p. 506. See also *ODNR*, no. 535, p. 427.

4. "John Fawcett," *Thespian Dictionary*; in the late eighteenth century his son John appeared on the New York stage (ibid.; Odell, *New York Stage*, I, 381). An exception to this casting was John Henry's performance as Damaetus in Charleston in 1774 (Willis, *Charleston Stage*, 68).

[31]
WHILE GENTLE PARTHENISA WALKS
(The Tender Husband)

(London: Jacob Tonson, 1705). [W&M micro]

"A Song sung by the Boy in *The Tender Husband.* Set by Mr. Daniel Purcell." S. sh. fol. (London: 1705); bass given. [CW photo from BM]

First performance: London, Drury Lane, 1705
First known American performance: New York, 1769

1. Steele was an essayist, author of political pamphlets, of plays, and at one time a comanager of Drury Lane; Winton, *Captain Steele*, 75; for instance, see letter of Richard Ambler of Virginia to his son Edward, September 25, 1748, in which Ambler advised his son at school in Wakefield, England, to read the *Spectator* for its style (Ambler Papers, CW micro 62-1). The periodicals were in many Virginia inventories.

2. Seilhamer, *History*, I, 281–82. See "The Modern Beau," no. 32, which was sung in the afterpiece, *The Honest Yorkshireman*, April 22, 1771, at Williamsburg.

3. See notes to "No Ice so hard," no. 43.

4. Ramondon was a bass singer and composer who flourished 1705–20. A tune of his, "All you that must take a leap in the dark," attained popularity as "Would I might be hanged," sung by Macheath in *The Beggar's Opera*.

5. Steele, *Occasional Verse*, ed. Blanchard, 83; Deutsch, *Handel*, 585–87.

6. John Wilks, the singing actor who originated the role of Clerimont, may have sung the song (Steele, *Occasional Verse*, ed. Blanchard, 120), although the 1705 single-sheet edition identifies the singer as "the Boy." "The Boy" was a term applied to vocalists with unchanged voices in the seventeenth- and early eighteenth-century theatres, who came on stage to perform songs as servants or in similar guises. Odell, *New York Stage*, I, 178.

[32]
THE MODERN BEAU
(The Honest Yorkshireman)

London: L. Gilliver, 1736. [W&M micro]

Henry Carey, *The Musical Century*, 3rd edn. (London: Printed for John Simpson, 1743); bass given. [CW photo from BM]

First performance: London, Haymarket, 1735
First known American performance: New York, 1752

1. Sonneck, *Early Opera*, 44.

2. "Set by the Author," as noted in the 1736 Gilliver edition; Lonsdale, *Dr. Charles Burney*, 25; Burney, *A General History*, II, 1000. Carey settled in London about 1710. His many songs were published in single-sheet form and in his collection, *The Musical Century*. Colonial playgoers heard his songs in *Love in a Village*, *Damon and Phillida*, *The Devil to Pay*, *The Provok'd Husband*, *The Miser*, and in his ballad operas, *The Contrivances* and *The Honest Yorkshireman*.

3. Hawkins, *A General History*, II, 827; "Henry Carey," *Grove V*. Possibly Linnert was the member of that name of the Stockholm Royal Orchestra who died in 1745. He quite probably was the Lawrence Westenzon Linart who was one of the five musicians in attendance at the arrival of Governor Robert Hunter in Jamaica in 1729 (Wright, *Revels*, 19).

4. Seilhamer, *History*, I, 149, New York, November 26, 1761; Quelch played Sapscull at the Haymarket, September 3, 1755, with Mrs. Quelch as Combrush (*LS*, pt. IV, I, 489); Seilhamer, *History*, I, 281–82, with *The Tender Husband*; Sonneck, *Early Opera*, 46; *Pennsylvania Packet*, November 23, 1772; *LDA*, July 29, 1748, at Twickenham.

[33]
MY PASSION IN VAIN
(The Maid of the Mill)

Bell, *British Theatre*, VIII; song text, p. 44 [W&M]

"Sung by Mr. Mattocks." *The Maid of the Mill*, a Comic Opera as perform'd at the Theatre Royal in Covent Garden, for Voice, Harpsichord, or Violin. (London: R. Bremner, 1765). [CW]

First performance: London, Covent Garden, 1765
First American performance: New York, 1769

1. Arnold (1740–1802; Doctor of Music, Oxford 1773) set a second song in the *Maid of the Mill* to another air by Cocchi; as theatre composer to Covent Garden and the Haymarket he produced forty-three operas, musical afterpieces, and pantomimes; he later was a noted organist and editor of the works of Handel. Hendrick, *Lees of Virginia*, 161.

2. Loewenberg, *Annals of Opera*, 1765, cols. 280–81; *VG*(PD), August 29, 1771.

3. The others were *Love in a Village*, *Thomas and Sally*, *The Padlock*, and *Lionel and Clarissa*. *The Maid of the Mill* was played in Annapolis September 20, 1771; the company appeared in Williamsburg before and after the Maryland engagement (Sonneck, *Early Opera*, 46).

4. Odell, *New York Stage*, I, 150–51, May 4, 1769; the "Dances incidental to the Opera" were mentioned in the bill; Pollock, *Philadelphia Theatre*, 25, 107; first act "read" June 23, 1769; Odell, *New York Stage*, I, 154.

[34]

SOLEMN DIRGE

(Romeo and Juliet)

Funeral Procession of Juliet and a "Solemn Dirge" added in Act V. Possibly based on Theophilus Cibber's revision of 1744, published December 10, 1748, "first revised in 1744 at the Haymarket, now acted at Drury Lane."

"A Compleat Score of the SOLEMN DIRGE in *Romeo and Juliet* as perform'd at the Theatre Royal in Covent Garden compos'd by Dr. Arne." (London: Printed for Henry Thorowgood, ca. 1765). [Royal College of Music microfilm]

First London performance (of Dirge): Covent Garden, 1750

First known American performance (of Dirge): Philadelphia, 1759

1. *LS*, pt. IV, I, 208, September 28, 1750; *Pennsylvania Gazette*, November 1, 1759, "with the Funeral Procession of Juliet to the Monument of the Capulets and a Solemn Dirge as it is perform'd at the Theatre Royal in Covent Garden"; *Maryland Gazette*, June 26, 1760.

2. *LS*, pt. IV, I, 208, September 28, 1750, and p. 209, October 1, 1750; Burney, *History*, II, 1010.

3. Boyce's setting of Garrick's text, apparently never published, is in the manuscript music attributed to him in the Bodleian Library (Cudworth, "Song and Part-Song Settings of Shakespeare's Lyrics," *Shakespeare in Music*, ed. Hartnoll, 62). Nicolo Pasquali composed music to the text of the Arne version, given February 18, 1754, at Sheridan's Smock Alley Theatre (Sheldon, *Thomas Sheridan*, 376). Charles Avison, the organist-composer, made a setting of Garrick's text (Cudworth, ibid.). Another setting of Garrick's text is in the manuscript music book that Francis Hopkinson of Philadelphia kept during 1759–60 (Charles Haywood, "William Boyce's 'Solemn Dirge' in Garrick's *Romeo and Juliet* production of 1750," *Shakespeare Quarterly*, XI [Spring, 1960], 173–85). Garrick's verses for the Drury Lane version of the dirge were printed in the Tonson edition of the play in 1750.

4. The surviving records of colonial performances show more frequent listings of the names of the vocal performers in *Romeo and Juliet* than they do in any of the other plays with choruses performed in the colonies. The number of singers listed in *Romeo and Juliet* bills varied from season to season, usually from five to seven, but once in 1768 only three were mentioned. The customary addition of "etc." at the end of the lists presumably allowed for the inclusion of other singers.

5. Handel transferred arias from one voice to another to take care of differences in changing casts (Deutsch, *Handel*, 177); Rosenfeld, *Strolling Players*, 25.

6. Nancy Hallam, as Mrs. Raynard, played Juliet in an American Company performance on July 1, 1775 at Kingston, Jamaica (Wright, *Revels*, 62), where the company had gone at the outbreak of the Revolution. She had married John Raynard, organist at Kingston Parish Church, on May 15, 1775 (Register of Kingston Marriages, 1753–1814, vol. 14, fol. 62, Spanish Town, Jamaica; courtesy of Mr. Clinton V. Black, archivist). Odell, *New York Stage*, I, 168, July 5, 1773.

7. The actors' presence that season is noted by entries in Washington's account book (Sonneck, *Early Concert Life*, 57) and by records of the Masonic Lodge (Kidd, *Early Freemasonry in Williamsburg, Virginia*, 9); *New York Mercury*, March 1, 1762.

[35]

LET'S SING OF STAGE COACHES

(The Stage Coach)

London: S. Curll and R. Franklin, 1718. [W&M micro]

"Mr. Doggett's Comical Song in the Farce of *The Stage Coach*, Sett by Mr. John Eccles and exactly engrav'd by D. Wright." *A Collection of Eighteenth-Century Single Sheet Songs*, III, 18; bass given; [*BU* date: London, 1706]. [FL]

First performance: London, Lincoln's Inn Fields, 1704

First known American performance: New York, 1750

1. So described by Captain Basil, Isabella's lover, who rushes to her rescue.

2. Thorp, *Songs from the Restoration Theatre*, 114; Pulver, *Biographical Dictionary of Old English Music*, 160–62.

3. Downes, *Roscius Anglicanus*, 52; Odell, *New York Stage*, I, 68, 57; Rosenfeld, *Strolling Players*, 277, 282. The English actor may have been Josias Miller (d. 1738). John Mottley, the dramatist, used Miller's name as a pseudonym for his *Joe Miller's Jest Book* ("Mottley," *DNB*). For Miller as Cymon, see "There's not a Swain," no. 27.

4. All of Farquhar's plays were in the colonial repertoire, the others being: *The Beaux' Stratagem*, *The Recruiting Officer*, *The Constant Couple*, *Sir Harry Wildair*, *Love and a Bottle*, *The Inconstant*, and *The Twin Rivals*; all had music in them. In "His Life and Character," prefixed to the 1718 edition of the play; Gray, *Theatrical Criticism*, 31, 32.

5. Two performances are recorded for Annapolis in 1760. The company was playing in Williamsburg from October 1760 through June 1761.

6. Middlesex County Will Book [B], 1713–34, 145, December 15, 1718, [VSL]; Fairfax County Will Book D-1, 1776–82, February 20, 1782 [VSL]. The estate of John Waller, justice and burgess, Spotsylvania County, included Farquhar's works, as well as a volume of *PPM*, in which Nicodemus's song was printed in the editions from 1707 through 1719 (Spotsylvania Will Book B, 1749–59, pp. 235–45 [VSL]). Thomas Jefferson owned the ninth edition of the works of "the late ingenuous Mr. George Farquhar," published in 1760 (LC, Jefferson Collection, *Catalogue*, ed. Sowerby, IV, 4587, p. 553). The *Virginia Gazette* advertised Farquhar's plays in three volumes for sale at the Williamsburg Printing Office in 1768 (*VG*(PD), February 28, 1768).

[36]

CUPID, GOD OF SOFT PERSUASION

(Love in a Village)

Bell, *British Theatre*, XIII, 1797. [W&M]

"Sung by Miss [Isabella] Hallam." *Love in a Village.* A comic opera as performed at the Theatre Royal in Covent Garden. The music by Handel, Boyce, Arne, Howard, Baildon, Festing, Geminiani, Galuppi, Giardini, Agus, Abos. For Harpsichord, Voice,

German Flute, or Violin.
London: J. Walsh, 1763.
[CW]

First performance: London, Covent Garden, 1762
First American performance: Charleston, 1766

1. Playbill, CW; Seilhamer, *History*, I, 278–79, 351; Charles Willson Peale was adjured to paint Maria Storer, "enchanting Maid," as Ariel in *The Tempest* (ibid., 281), a role supplied with songs and one her mother had played in Dublin (Sheldon, *Thomas Sheridan*, 467–68).

2. *VG*(R), December 3, 1772, "Just publish'd, to be sold by Edward Cumins at the Printing Office... Price, One Pistereen"; "*The Storer*, a Song-book" was also advertised in *VG*(D), August 24, 1776, and January 17, 1777; *VG*(PD), February 25, 1768.

3. *LS*, pt. IV, II, 967. According to a description supplied through the kindness of Mr. W. N. H. Harding, who has a copy in his collection, *The Brent* is a 12 mo volume of 344 pages containing more than four hundred songs performed at the London theatres and pleasure gardens. Nearly all of them are given with the names of the performers who sang them, and of the plays in which they were sung. Other songs from plays in the colonial repertoire are included.

4. Description courtesy of Mr. Harding, who suggests that the use of "Syren" in the titles of the songbooks named in honor of various singing-actresses of the period may have been influenced by a song by Ambrose Phillips, "The little Syren of the Stage," which attained great popularity about 1730.

5. Odell, *New York Stage*, I, 122, January 8, 1768, Maria Storer's first New York singing appearance. For other appearances, see ibid., 127, 132, 150–53; Pollock, *Philadelphia Theatre*, 104.

6. Loewenberg, *Annals of Opera*, "Love in a Village," 1762, cols. 266–67; Burney, *A General History*, II, 896; John W. Molnar, "A Collection of Music in Colonial Virginia: The Ogle Inventory," *MQ*, XLIX, no. 2 (April, 1963), 158.

[37]
MY DOLLY WAS THE FAIREST THING
(Love in a Village)

Bell, *British Theatre*, XIII, 1797. [W&M]

"Sung by Mr. Beard."
Air adapted from Handel, "Let me wander not unseen," from *L'Allegro, il Penseroso, ed il Moderato*; score of opera: see "Cupid, God of soft Persuasion." [CW]

First performance: London, Covent Garden, 1762
First American performance: Charleston, 1766

1. First performed February 27, 1740; the third part, *Il Moderato*, written by Jennens (Deutsch, *Handel*, 496); Maria Storer sang the original air with two other Handel arias at a concert in New York in 1769 (Odell, *New York Stage*, I, 152). Handel, German-born composer and naturalized Briton, was pre-eminent in England in opera, oratorio, and concerts; his songs and instrumental compositions were owned by Virginians; the music-loving governor of Virginia, Francis Fauquier (1704–68), had been on the board of the Foundling Hospital with Handel in London, and had discussed with him performances of *Messiah* (Deutsch, *Handel*, 752–53; *LDA*, May 14, 1752). After the Revolution (1790) Maria Storer, by then the third Mrs. Henry, appeared in Philadelphia in a concert featuring Handel's songs with the Rev. Benjamin Blagrave of Virginia, a singing clergyman and son-in-law of Peter Pelham, the organist at Bruton Parish Church in Williamsburg (Sonneck, *Early Concert Life*, 119). Some years earlier (1785) her singing of selections from *Messiah* at the close of a church service in Charleston had shocked Noah Webster (Willis, *Charleston Stage*, 93).

2. Irving, *John Gay*, 242. Pepusch arranged the music for *The Beggar's Opera*.

3. Beard sang in a performance of *L'Allegro* at the Concert Room (formerly Ogle's) in Dean Street in 1759, the year Handel died (Deutsch, *Handel*, 811–12, March 1, 1759); Pollock, *Philadelphia Theatre*, 21; Willis, *Charleston Stage*, 49; Loewenberg, *Annals of Opera*, cols. 266–67, December 8, 1762, Covent Garden; Sonneck, *Early Opera*, 33–34.

4. Pollock, *Philadelphia Theatre*, 21; playbill, CW; Hallam conducted the orchestra for *Comus* in Philadelphia on March 8, 1770 (Sonneck, *Early Opera*, 24), and for *Lionel and Clarissa* in Philadelphia on December 14, 1772 (*Pennsylvania Packet*, December 14, 1772).

5. *VG*(PD), May 23, 1771; ibid., May 16, 1771. Russworm, "a worthy, good tempered man, who played such a sweet fiddle," was drowned two years later (ibid., June 24, 1773).

6. Kimball, *Jefferson: The Road to Glory*, 55, from Jefferson's own account. Alberti(e) had advertised to teach violin in Philadelphia during the American Company's first season after their arrival from Jamaica. According to Jefferson, Alberti taught him in Williamsburg and at Monticello. Sonneck, *Francis Hopkinson and James Lyon*, 23; Philip Ludwell Lee to his brother William in London, July 25, 1771, manuscript letter, Philip Ludwell Lee Letters, VHS; Leonard's name was connected in New York concerts with the instrumentalists and singers of the American Company (Odell, *New York Stage*, I, 95–98; Sonneck, *Early Concert Life*, 166–69); *VG*(PD), September 21, 1776; playbill, CW. Maria Storer's elder sister, Ann, the then Mrs. Henry, also was among the servants in the cast.

[38]
IF EVER I'M CATCH'D
(Love in a Village)

Bell, *British Theatre*, XIII, 1797. [W&M]

"Sung by Mr. Beard."
Score: see "Cupid, God of soft Persuasion," no. 36.

First performance: London, Covent Garden, 1762
First American performance: Charleston, 1766

1. Thorp, *Songs from the Restoration Theatre*, 87, "Fiddle's Song, 'In Praise of Country Life,'" in Shadwell's *Epsom Wells* (1672), set by Robert Smith (1648–75).

2. Colonial theatregoers heard Boyce's music in his little opera *The Chaplet* and in *The Roman Father*, *The Orphan*, *Love in a Village*, and *Lethe*.

3. *Virginia Gazette*, Royle Daybook, June 16, 1764; *VG*(PD), November 29, 1770, and August 29, 1771; Campbell was an alderman of Norfolk Borough 1791–93 (*Lower Norfolk County Virginia Antiquary*, I (1895), 29–30, 60); after the Revolution, Tucker was a noted jurist and professor of law at the College of William and Mary; letter to St. George Tucker, September 24, 1772, Tucker-Coleman Collection, W&M; Robert Carter Letter Book, 1770–73, VHS.

[39]

ALLY CROAKER

(The Buck, or The Englishman in Paris)

London: P. Vaillant, 1753. (Song text not printed in play.) [W&M micro]	"A New Song," *The Universal Magazine*, XIII (1753), 174; bass given. [HL]

First performance: London, Covent Garden, 1753
First known American performance: Williamsburg, 1771

1. Playbill, CW. Foote, actor, manager, and playwright, wrote a number of lampoons he called "petit pieces." Those seen in colonial America were *Taste*, *Fanny the Phantom*, (the second part of *Orators*), and *The Mayor of Garrat*.

2. Gamut was played by Stephen Woolls in colonial performances.

3. Belden, *Samuel Foote*, 67; Appleton, *Macklin*, 95; *LS*, pt. IV, II, 859, Covent Garden, April 21, 1761.

4. Belden, *Samuel Foote*, 120, 151 ff.; "Samuel Foote," *Thespian Dictionary*; "English Guitar," *Grove V*; Marcuse, *Musical Instruments: A Comprehensive Dictionary*, 172; the "English" guitar was smaller than the present-day Spanish guitar, and was strung and tuned differently; Washington's stepdaughter, Patsy Custis, possessed one of the first known instructors [lesson books] for the guitar, issued in 1758 by Robert Bremner, the Edinburgh and London music publisher (Howard, *Music of George Washington's Time*, 16); Nancy, the thirteen-year-old daughter of Councilor Carter of Nomini Hall played the instrument (Fithian, *Journal*, 28, 36, 42); her cousin Lucy, youngest daughter of Col. Landon Carter, received lessons from Giovanni Gualdo in 1767 (*Landon Carter Diary*, ed. Greene, I, 336); Gualdo later figured prominently in the musical activities of Philadelphia until his death in 1772 (Sonneck, *Early Concert Life*, 66, 70–74). In addition to the guitar, Miss Hallam accompanied herself in various roles on the harpsichord or spinet.

5. Willis, *Charleston Stage*, 50; handbills bearing Wall's advertisement to teach at Albany, New York, CW; Odell, *New York Stage*, I, 142, 153, 175; Wall also played the guitar on the stage (see "Dear Heart, what a terrible Life am I led," no. 40) and accompanied Miss Wainwright on the guitar in a song between the acts of *The Country Lasses*, April 18, 1768 (ibid., 132, 175).

6. *LS*, pt. IV, I, 385, Drury Lane, October 20, 1753; Chappell, *Popular Music of the Olden Time*, ed. Sternfeld, II, 713–14, attributed the words of "Ally Croaker" to Samuel Foote. The first edition of the play (London: Vaillant, 1753) published before the Drury Lane production (*LS*, pt. IV, I, 360), printed verses in French for Lucinda's song that have no connection with the text of "Ally Croaker." Chappell found a resemblance to "Ally Croaker" in a song used by Cibber in his *Love in a Riddle* (1729). *BU* lists single-sheet editions of words and music in the 1730s and 1740s.

[40]

DEAR HEART, WHAT A TERRIBLE LIFE AM I LED

(The Padlock)

Inchbald, *Collection of Farces and Other Afterpieces*, IV [W&M]	"Sung by Mr. Dibdin in the Character of Mungo." *The Padlock*. A Comic Opera as it is perform'd at the Theatre Royal in Drury Lane. London, J. Johnson, 1768; score. [CW]

First performance: London, Drury Lane, 1768
First American performance: New York, 1769

1. Bickerstaffe took his story from Cervantes's *El Celoso extremeno* (Loewenberg, *Annals of Opera*, 1768, col. 303); Pedicord, *Theatrical Public*, 148).

2. Southern, *Changeable Scenery*, 237, illustration opp. p. 304; Odell, *New York Stage*, I, 151; four performances were recorded in the first two and a half weeks after it was introduced, May 29, 1769, and over three dozen in the following five years.

3. Seilhamer, *History*, I, 249; ibid., 300; Mungo was played in the nineteenth century by the American Negro actor Ira Aldridge (1804–67).

4. Dibdin, a singing actor, composer to Covent Garden, and theatre historian, was a prolific and popular song writer; many of his sea songs were published in collections well into the nineteenth century; *VG*(PD), January 26, 1769; the song "When a Woman's Front is wrinkl'd" had been printed in the J. Johnson edition of the opera, London, 1768 (*BU*, I, 753); colonial theatregoers heard Dibdin's music in *The Padlock*, *Lionel and Clarissa*, and *The Maid of the Mill*.

5. Playbill, CW; afterpiece to *The Clandestine Marriage*. This is the first known performance in Williamsburg of *The Padlock*, but possibly it had been played earlier. The company performed the same combination of main and afterpiece in New York in 1773 (Odell, *New York Stage*, I, 160, April 19, 1773); *VG*(PD), November 29, 1770; August 28, 1771.

6. Pollock, *Philadelphia Theatre*, 131.

[41]

YE MORTALS WHOM FANCIES AND TROUBLES PERPLEX

(Lethe)

London: P. Vaillant, 1749. [W&M micro]	"A Song in *Lethe*, Sung by Mr. Beard in the Character of Mercury," *Gentleman's Magazine*, XIX (July, 1749), 323; bass given. [CW]

First performance: London, Drury Lane, 1740
First known American performance: New York, 1751

1. Based on Boursault's *Les Fables d'Esope* (Knapp, "Garrick's Last Command Performance," *The Age of Johnson*, ed. Hilles, 63). A type of dramatic satire involving Aesop and the judgment of current follies in the manner of Lucian was popular in the period (Hughes, *A Century of Farce*, 126).

2. In classical mythology, Lethe was a river of Hades whose waters when drunk caused forgetfulness of the past.

3. Garrick, *Letters*, xxxii, xxxiv, and plate opposite 148 (illustration of the playbill for the Ipswich performance); Nagler, *Source Book*, 361; more than thirty-seven performances were recorded in the colonies from 1751 through 1774; "William Boyce," *Grove III*.

4. Odell, *New York Stage*, I, 55; ibid., 44, December 23, 1751. Garrick's plays performed in the colonies included *Lethe*, *Miss in Her Teens*, *The Irish Widow*, *Catherine and Petruccio*, *Cymon*, *The Guardian*, *The Lying Valet*, *Neck or Nothing*, and *The Clandestine Marriage* (with George Colman).

5. *New York Mercury*, December 3, 1753; *VG*, August 28, 1752. After the Revolution Lewis Hallam, Jr., resumed his career in America as an actor and manager; he died in 1808, aged 68.

6. *New York Mercury*, December 3, 1753; Odell, *New York Stage*, I, 88, February 1, 1762; *LS*, pt. IV, I, Drury Lane, May 13, 1751 and May 16, 1754; ibid., pt. IV, II, Drury Lane, season of 1756–57; Rosenfeld, *Strolling Players*, 279; Odell, *New York Stage*, I, 115; *Pennsylvania Packet*, January 25, 1773.

[42]

SHE WALKS AS SHE DREAMS

(Alexander the Great)

London: J. Magnes & R. Bentley, 1677. [W&M micro]	"Sung by Mr. Pate in the Opera of *Alexander the Great*, Set by Mr. D. Purcell." (From the dialogue, beginning "Is Innocence so void of Care") s. sh. fol., (London: ca. 1700); bass given. [CW Krummel Collection, BM, photo]

First performance: London, Drury Lane, 1677
First known American performance: Philadelphia, 1768

1. Cibber, *Apology*, I, 105.

2. Nettleton, *English Drama*, 96, 99; Cibber, *Apology*, I, 113–14 and fn.; "Nathaniel Lee," *DNB*; "Nathaniel Lee," *OCEL*; *LS*, pt. I, lxxxi, 291; Lee, *Theodosius, or The Force of Love* (London: R. Bentley and M. Magnes, 1680) [W&M micro]; *LS*, pt. I, cxxl–cxxli; *ESB* has twenty-three of Lee's songs indexed under the author, p. 412.

3. *RMA Research Chronicle No. 1*, ed. Tilmouth, 90, April 26, 1715; CW, Krummel photostat, "In the Opera of *Alexander the Great*"; *LS*, pt. II, I, 69, Drury Lane, June 13, 1704; *ESB*, no. 190, p. 123; no. 1836, p. 267.

4. Garrick, *Letters*, no. 329, p. 411; Gray, *Theatrical Criticism*, 166; Pollock, *Philadelphia Theatre*, 332, April 3, 1797; Rosenfeld, *Strolling Players*, 151.

5. Seilhamer, *History*, I, 242, 249. Willis, *Charleston Stage*, 73, February 10, 1774 (presented with *Miller of Mansfield* during the American Company's final colonial season); during the period of Williamsburg's first theatre seventeen performances are recorded at Lincoln's Inn Fields between March 16, 1717, and November 14, 1727 (*LS*, pt. II, I and II, 441–944).

6. Odell, *New York Stage*, I, 88, February 4, 1762; Pollock, *Philadelphia Theatre*, 105 (performance at Southwark Theatre, Philadelphia, December 30, 1768). William Pate, identified on the single-sheet folio as the ghost singer, was a well-known concert and theatre vocalist whom John Evelyn in 1698 described as "reputed the most excellent singer ever England had" (*LS*, pt. I, 496).

[43]

NO ICE SO HARD, SO COLD, AS I

(Miss in Her Teens)

London: Printed for J. and R. Tonson, 1747. [W&M micro]	"Sung by Mr. Dodd in the Character of Fribble, in *Miss in Her Teens*." Score in *Thalia, a Collection of Six Favourite Songs* (London: John Johnston, ca. 1767). [BM]

First performance: London, Covent Garden, 1747
First American performance: New York, 1751

1. Seilhamer, *History*, I, 236 (with *The Drummer*); the following year the company gave it with *The Beggar's Opera* at Annapolis on May 18, 1769 (ibid., 260); it is recorded in the Murray-Kean repertoire, in the Hallam Company's original play stock, and in nearly every season of the American Company.

2. Garrick, *Letters*, no. 30, p. 47; ibid, no. 50, p. 88n; Dryden had ridiculed the contemporary stage beau who "tickled the Eyes but not the Ears" (Barker, *Mr. Cibber*, 28); Scholes, *The Great Dr. Burney*, 368; England, *Garrick's Jubilee*, 40.

3. The song text is printed in the 1747 Tonson edition, and retained in that of Inchbald, *Farces*, IV, (1808).

4. Pollock, *Philadelphia Theatre*, 75, 115; Willis, *Charleston Stage*, 49, 50, 85, 108; Odell, *New York Stage*, I, 122; ibid., 134–36, May 2, 1768, repeated May 23; Clark, *Irish Stage*, 89; Sheldon, *Thomas Sheridan*, 441–42, March 15, 1749. She also played Biddy (May 26, 1757) as did at least two of her daughters: "Miss Storer" at Smock Alley, October 24, 1757, when Miss A. Storer and Miss E. Storer are listed in the company; Maria Storer also played Biddy (*Pennsylvania Packet*, April 16, 1773); Ann, the eldest surviving daughter, played Biddy as "Miss Storer from the Theatre in Jamaica" at her Philadelphia debut, October 6, 1767 (Seilhamer, *History*, I, 199).

[44]

BILLY PRINGLE'S PIG

(The Mayor of Garrat)

London: P. Vaillant, 1769. (Song not printed in play.) [W&M micro]	"Sung with great Applause in *The Mayor of Garrat*." S. sh. fol., (London: Printed at the Little a, Leadenhall Street [ca. 1780]); bass given. [BM]

First performance of play: London, Haymarket, 1763; song interpolated 1771
First known American performance: Philadelphia, 1767

1. *LS*, pt. IV, III, 1563.

2. *ODNR*, no. 42, pp. 73–74; the song was printed (with variations in the the title, of "Betty" or "Billy") into the nineteenth century; in 1805, in *Songs for the Nursery*, "Johnny Pringle" reappeared in the title; Belden, *Samuel Foote*, 171.

3. Fitzgerald, *Samuel Foote*, 260; the tune to "An Old Woman Cloath'd in Gray" was used for Air 1 in *The Beggar's Opera*; the song, "Johnny Pringle" is mentioned by Weston in Garrick's play, *The Meeting of the Company* (1774), in which Weston played himself (Stein, *Three Garrick Plays*, 144); Weston was still featured as Sneak with the "Song of Johnny Pringle" at Drury Lane on April 22, 1775, less than a year before his death (*LS*, pt. IV, III, 1885); Rosenfeld, *Strolling Players*, 298–99.

4. *ODNR*, no. 42, pp. 73–74; Fitzgerald, *Samuel Foote*, 292; *Gentleman's Magazine*, XXXVI (1766), 295; "Sir John Pringle," *DNB*.

5. "If ever a fond Inclination," another minuet by Geminiani, was used in *Love in a Village* and is among the music in Mrs. Thomas Jefferson's collection. Geminiani's music also was heard in the colonies in *Beau in the Suds* and *Don Quixote in England*. Jefferson owned Geminiani's *Rules for Playing in a true Taste on the Violin . . . Opera VIII* (London: ca. 1739) and *The Art of Playing on the Violin, Opera IX* (London: 1751), LC, Jefferson Collection, *Catalogue*, ed. Sowerby, IV, no. 4255, p. 405; *VG*, October 21, 1737, "From the *London Magazine*," which had Virginia subscribers.

6. Cross, *Henry Fielding*, I, 156; Belden, *Samuel Foote*, 178; mock elections were held annually during the first half of the eighteenth century at the town of Garrat, Surrey.

7. Pollock, *Philadelphia Theatre*, 92, 98; Willis, *Charleston Stage*, 50; "Morris, Owen" (1719–1809), *Grove III, Supplement*, 8; Pollock, *Philadelphia Theatre*, 115, 123, November 11, 1772, and February 8, 1773; Nagler, *Source Book*, 516.

[45]

ATTEND, ALL YE FAIR

(The Way to Keep Him)

Three-act version (London: P. Vaillant, 1760) [W&M micro]; five-act version [1762] Bell, *British Theatre* (1797), XVII [W&M]; song text in both editions	"A Song sung by Miss Macklin in *The Way to Keep Him*." The *Universal Magazine*, XXVI, first supplement (1760), 372; bass given. [HL]

First performance: London, Drury Lane, 1759
First American performance: Charleston, 1766

1. *Gentleman's Magazine*, XXX (1760) 40, 68–74; *Universal Magazine* (see source notation); both periodicals had Virginia subscribers; the February issue of the former advertised the Vaillant edition of the play (1760) under "Lists of Books Publish'd."

2. *VG*(PD), April 23, 1772; the play was given by the New American Company (known as the Virginia Company the year before) with Mrs. Osborne as the widow and William Verling as Lovemore in Annapolis on May 23, 1769 (Seilhamer, *History*, I, 263); *Pennsylvania Packet*, November 23, 1772; Seilhamer, *History*, I, 317, April 14, 1773.

3. The other six were: *The Orphan of China*, *The Old Maid*, *The Upholsterer*, *The Apprentice*, *All in the Wrong*, and *The Citizen*; copies of the last named and of two others not recorded in the colonial repertoire, *No One's Enemy but his Own* and *What we must all Come to*, were sold at the Printing Office in Williamsburg (Royle Daybook, June 16 and July 9, 1764).

4. *Music in the Huntington Library*, ed. Backus, 316; *LS*, pt. IV, III, 1562, 1863; *BU*, II, 957, "Adam Smith"; songs sung at the Grotto Gardens were published in a collection: *Brewster's Vauxhall and Grotto songs*, which were advertised for sale in Williamsburg (*VG*(PD), September 17, 1772).

5. Arne's song was "Ye Fair Married Dames." The original song was retained; on March 24, 1768, at Covent Garden, Maria Macklin was Widow Bellmour "with the Original Song"; two weeks later, April 6, 1768, at Drury Lane, Mrs. Abington was the widow "with a Song in Character" (*LS*, pt. IV, III, 1320, 1321); Oman, *David Garrick*, 137.

[46]

WOULD YOU WITH HER YOU LOVE BE BLEST

(The Oracle)

London: R. and J. Dodsley, 1763. [W&M micro]	*Vocal Melody*, Book IV (London: Printed for J. Walsh, 1752); bass given. [CW]

First performance: London, Covent Garden, 1752
First American performance: Charleston, 1766

1. A fourth verse (an appeal to the audience) was printed in the play text but not in the music score; it is omitted here.

2. Ashley, *Colley Cibber*, 152. Susannah, second wife of Theophilus Cibber, sang in Handel's operas and oratorios.

3. *VG*(PD), April 23, 1772.

4. Sheldon, *Thomas Sheridan*, 446. Performances of *The Oracle* "all by children" are noted elsewhere (*LS*, pt. IV, I, 360, March 24, 1753, Covent Garden, and others).

5. Willis, *Charleston Stage*, 51–53; Seilhamer, *History*, I, 278–80; Miss Hallam and the song were featured in the bills (Pollock, *Philadelphia Theatre*, 86, December 5, 1766; p. 88, January 2, and p. 95, March 28, 1767; p. 108, September 30, 1769); letter printed in *Maryland Gazette*, September 6, 1770; Seilhamer, *History*, I, 278.

6. Odell, *New York Stage*, I, 119, December 14, 1767.

[47]

LONG HAVE I BEEN WITH GRIEF OPPREST

(The Female Parson, or Beau in the Suds)

London: L. Gilliver and F. Cogan, 1730. [W&M micro]	Air, "My Bonny Jean," melody only, printed with play text (London: Gilliver and Cogan, 1730). [W&M micro]

First performance: London, Haymarket, 1730
First known American performance: New York, 1750

1. There were only two London performances: April 27 and 30, 1730, at the Haymarket (*LS*, pt. III, I, 55–56); Odell, *New York Stage*, I, 34, 37, 42; *Maryland Gazette*, July 16 and 30, 1752; *VG*, September 26 and October 24, 1751; April 17, 1752; the *Maryland Gazette* of June 18, 1752, announced the arrival of the company at Annapolis fromVirginia.

2. Johnson, *Scots Musical Museum*, I, 55, and II, 57.

3. Ibid.; for another tune in *The Beau in the Suds*, see "O All ye Powers above," no. 8.

4. *The Beau in the Sudds*, or *Suds* (Odell, *New York Stage*, I, 34, 37–38, 42); the phrase meant to be in difficulties, embarrassed, disgraced, or perplexed.

[48]

THE ROMP'S SONG

(The Provok'd Husband)

The Dramatic Works of Colley Cibber, Esq. (London: J. Rivington and Sons, 1777) IV, 103–216; song text, 184	"The Romp," sung by Mrs. Cibber in *The Provok'd Husband*, words and music by Mr. Carey, *A Collection of Eighteenth-Century Single Sheet Songs*, III, 112; bass given; [*BU* date: London, ca. 1735]. [FL]

First performance: London, Drury Lane, 1728
First known American performance: New York, 1752

1. Barker, *Mr. Cibber*, 146; Cross, *Henry Fielding*, I, 61; *LS*, pt. II, II, 954, cast of 1728 edition.

2. *LS*, pt. II, II, 970, April 11, 1728. The performance was for the benefit of Theophilus Cibber and Mrs. Cibber. Jennie's role was billed at Drury Lane "with the Proper Songs" [i.e., the songs belonging to the part] for many years afterwards (for example, *LS*, pt. III, II, 1277, Drury Lane, January 3, 1747 and *LS*, pt. IV, II, 723 Drury Lane, April 27, 1759); both songs were printed in the second edition of the play published by J. Watts in 1729, and are in the 1777 edition (*The Dramatic Works of Colley Cibber*, IV, 209).

3. See "The Epilogue Song," no. 50.

4. Mrs. Harman and her uncle, Theophilus Cibber, are listed as acting during the 1756–57 season at minor London playhouses (*LS*, pt. IV, II, 1756–57 season); "The sensible, humane, and benevolent" Mrs. Harman, "who possessed much merit in low comedy," died in New York on May 27, 1773 (Seilhamer, *History*, I, 321; Pollock, *Philadelphia Theatre*, 30). She doubled in the part of Lady Grace in this and other Philadelphia performances (ibid., 78, 80, 82); more than twenty-one recorded performances show that in addition to being in the Murray-Kean repertoire it was in the Hallam Company's original play stock in 1752–54, the Virginia-New American Company gave it in 1768–69, and the regular company's repertoire included it for all the seasons when it played the Virginia-Maryland circuit; *VG*(PD), April 21, 1772 with *Thomas and Sally* (see "The Echoing Horn," no. 49); playbill for Tuesday, May 22, 1771, "to be added, *Love a-la-Mode*," CW.

[49]

THE ECHOING HORN

(Thomas and Sally, or The Sailor's Return)

The text is in the score.	"A Musical Entertainment as it is performed at the Theatre Royal in Covent Garden. The Second Edition." Complete score (London: Printed for G. Kearsley, 1763). [CW]

First performance: Covent Garden, 1760
First known American performance: Philadelphia, 1766

1. Priscilla Dawson was the widow of the Rev. Thomas Dawson, who died in 1761; both he and his brother William were presidents of the College of William and Mary; August 21, 1769, Blair, Banister, Braxton, Horner, and Whiting Papers, Earl Gregg Swem Library, W&M.

2. Baines, *Woodwind Instruments*, 298; Loewenberg, *Annals of Opera*, 1760, col. 249.

3. *VG*(PD), May 23, 1771; Sonneck, *Early Concert Life*, 70; *VG*(R), December 11, 1766; ibid., December 24, 1767; Sonneck, *Early Concert Life*, 22, 170, 181 (spelled "Humphrey" and "Humphries"); Rendall, *The Clarinet*, 80; Odell, *New York Stage*, I, 96, March 26, 1764 and April 17, 1764; Sonneck, *Early Concert Life*, 71–73. Stadler taught in the homes of the Washington, Lee, Carter, and other Virginia families; according to Philip Fithian, he was an excellent flautist (Fithian, *Journal*, 82); Odell, *New York Stage*, I, 167, 169; Pollock, *Philadelphia Theatre*, 101.

4. Playbill of June 20, 1770 (with *The Clandestine Marriage*), CW; the other three members of the cast were: Thomas, John Henry; Dorcas, Mrs. Harman; and Sally, Miss Nancy Hallam. Washington, *Diaries*, ed. Fitzpatrick, I, 384; Seilhamer, *History*, I, 259; *VG*(PD), April 16, 1772. Mrs. Stamper, a singer with the company, made one of her rare appearances as an actress as Dorcas; the remainder of the cast was the same as that listed on the playbill of June 20, 1770; Pollock, *Philadelphia Theatre*, 85.

5. Odell, *New York Stage*, I, 117; Nagler, *Source Book*, 516; *VG*(PD), October 18, 1770, supplement. "Then the Service began and an anthem, accompanied by the organ was sung, conducted by Mr. Woolls," who probably secured singers and arranged for the music. Woolls, said to have been born in Bath, England, died in 1799 in New York.

[50]

EPILOGUE SONG

(The Irish Widow)

London: T. Beckett, 1772. [W&M micro]	"Epilogue to the *Irish Widow* Sung by Mrs. Barry Compos'd by J. Vernon." S. sh. fol. (London: J. Johnston, 1772), bass given. [BM]

First performance: London, Drury Lane, 1772
First American performance: New York, 1773

1. The epilogue to a play, *Caligula*, in 1698 observed that "singing in Plays is grown so much in vogue I had some thought to sing an Epilogue" (*LS*, pt. 1, cxviii). Musical epilogues to plays were not unusual in the eighteenth century; among them were one for *Love in a Riddle*, 1729, and an unperformed one written by Goldsmith for *She Stoops to Conquer*, 1773 (Goldsmith, *Collected Works*, V, 392–93).

2. Cudworth, "Settings of Shakespeare's Lyrics," *Shakespeare in Music*, ed. Hartnoll, 67; "Joseph Vernon," *Grove III*; "Joseph Vernon," *BMB*; Joseph Vernon, "The Celebrated Epilogue in the Comedy of Twelfth Night," in *New Songs in the Pantomime of The Witches*, (London: J. Johnston, 1772 [*BU*, II, 1039]); *The Witches*, an afterpiece by James Love, was given in the colonies from 1767 to 1774 (Seilhamer, *History*, I, 154, 169, 213, 249, 332).

3. Garrick, *Letters*, no. 96, p. 156–67, fn. 1; no. 419, p. 530, fn. 5; no. 706, p. 817; no. 720, p. 832–33; Clark, *Irish Stage*, 350.

4. First American performance, Odell, *New York Stage*, I, 168; Wright, *Revels*, 77, 157.

5. Wood, *Personal Recollections*, 26; "Charlotte Morris" (1753–1826), *Oxford Companion to the Theatre*; playbill, May 1, 1771, *Love in a Village*, with Mrs. Morris as Margery, CW; "Owen Morris," *Grove III, American Supplement*. The Morrises had parts in the last play to be performed in Philadelphia in the eighteenth century: on December 30, 1799. In the large cast they were the only actors who had performed on the colonial stage. In addition to the play, a monody with vocal and instrumental music was given in memory of George Washington, who had died two weeks earlier (Pollock, *Philadelphia Theatre*, 403; Seilhamer, *History*, I, 353).

Bibliography

1. MUSIC

ARNE, THOMAS A. *Artaxerxes*, An English Opera as it is perform'd at the Theatre Royal in Covent Garden. Set to music by Dr. Arne. Printed for the Author, 1762. [CW]

——. "The Serenade." Sung by Mr. Mattocks in *The Merchant of Venice*. S. sh. fol. London: ca. 1770. [BM]

——. A Complete Score of the "Solemn Dirge" in *Romeo and Juliet* as perform'd at the Theatre Royal in Covent Garden compos'd by Dr. Arne. London: Printed for Henry Thorowgood, ca. 1765. [Royal College of Music, London]

——. *Thomas and Sally*. A Musical Entertainment as it is performed at the Theatre Royal in Covent Garden. 2nd edn. London: Printed for G. Kearsley, 1763. [CW]

——. Dirge in *Cymbeline*. S. sh. fol. London: ca. 1760. [BM]

ARNE, THOMAS A. AND OTHERS. *Love in a Village*. A Comic Opera as it is perform'd at the Theatre Royal in Covent Garden. The music by Handel, Boyce, Arne, Howard, Baildon, Festing, Geminiani, Galuppi, Agus, Abos. For Harpsichord, Voice, German flute, or Violin. London: J. Walsh, 1763. [CW]

ARNOLD, SAMUEL, AND OTHERS. *The Maid of the Mill*, a Comic Opera as perform'd at the Theatre Royal in Covent Garden, for Voice, Harpsichord, or Violin. London: R. Bremner, 1765. [CW]

BAILDON, JOSEPH. Jessica's Song in *The Merchant of Venice*. S. sh. fol. London: 1770. [BM]

BICKHAM, GEORGE. *The Musical Entertainer*. 2 vols. London: G. Bickham, 1740. [CW]

BROWNLOW, WILLIAM, compiler[?]. *Midas*. A Comic Opera. Harpsichord, Voice, German Flute, or Guitar. Sung by Miss Hallam, Miss Miller, Miss Poitier, Mr. Beard, Mr. Mattocks, and Mr. Fawcett. London: Printed for J. Walsh, 1764. [CW]

CAREY, HENRY. *The Musical Century*. 3rd edn. London: Printed for John Simpson, 1743. [CW photo from BM]

A Collection of Eighteenth-Century Single Sheet Songs. Bound in 4 volumes. [FL]

[Composer unidentified]. "Balin a mone," sung by Mr. Barington [*sic*] in *The Double Disappointment*. S. sh. fol. London: ca. 1750. [University of Glasgow]

[Composer unidentified]. "Love's a sweet and soft Musician." A Favourite Song in *The Musical Lady*. S. sh. fol. London: ca. 1775. [BM]

DIBDIN, CHARLES. *The Padlock*. A Comic Opera as it is perform'd at the Theatre Royal in Drury Lane. London: J. Johnson, 1768. [CW]

GEMINIANI, FRANCESCO. "The Tragical History of the Life and Death of Billy Pringle's Pig," Sung with Great Applause in *The Mayor of Garrat*. S. sh. fol. London: Printed at the Little a, Leadenhall Street, [ca. 1780]. [BM]

Krummel Collection of Eighteenth-Century Single Sheet Songs in the British Museum. [CW from BM]

LAWES, WILLIAM. "Wher' did you borrow that last Sigh?" Autograph score. [BM, Add. Mss. 31432]

[LEVERIDGE, RICHARD]. *The Original Songs, Airs, and Choruses which were introduced into the Tragedy of Macbeth* in Score, by Matthew Locke, revised and corrected by Dr. Boyce. London: Longman and Broderip, ca. 1780. [CW]

PURCELL, DANIEL. "Sabina with an Angel's Face." Sung by Mr. Leveridge, Sett by Mr. Daniell Purcell. S. sh. fol. London: 1707. [Birmingham, England, Public Library]

——. "She walks as she dreams." Sung by Mr. Pate in the Opera of *Alexander the Great*. S. sh. fol. London: ca. 1700. [Krummel Collection, CW]

——. "The Serenading Song." Sung by Mr. Freeman in *The Constant Couple*. S. sh. fol. London: 1700. [CW]

——. "While gentle Parthenisa walks." A Song sung by the Boy in *The Tender Husband*, set by Mr. Daniel Purcell. S. sh. fol. London: 1705. [Shakespeare Memorial Library, Birmingham, England]

PURCELL, HENRY. *Orpheus Britannicus*. A Collection of All the Choicest Songs for 1, 2, and 3 Voices compos'd by Mr. Henry Purcell. London: Printed by J. Heptinstall for Henry Playford, 1698. [CW]

SEEDO, ———. "Ye Gods, Ye gave to me a Wife." S. sh. fol. London: 1732. [BM]

Songs in the Farce call'd The Mock Doctor. London: Printed and sold at the Musick Shops [1732]. [BM]

Thalia, a Collection of Six Favourite Songs. London: John Johnston, ca. 1760. [BM]

The Universal Harmony. London: Printed for J. Newbery, 1745. [CW]

VERNON, JOSEPH. "Epilogue to *The Irish Widow*" Sung by Mrs. Barry. S. sh. fol. London: J. Johnston, 1772. [BM]

Vocal Melody. Book IV. London: Printed for J. Walsh, 1752. [CW]

WATTS, JOHN. *The Musical Miscellany*. 6 volumes. London: J. Watts, 1729–31. [CW]

2. PRIMARY SOURCES

A. Manuscript

AMBLER, ELIZABETH BARBOUR. Papers. Alderman Library of the University of Virginia, Charlottesville. CW microfilm.

Blair, Banister, Braxton, Horner, and Whiting Papers. Earl Gregg Swem Library, W&M.
Carter, Robert (of Nomini Hall). Letter books: 1764–68, CW; 1771–73, VHS.
Chesterfield County, Va., Will Book, I, 1749–65. VSL.
Dawson Papers, 1728–75. LC.
Fairfax County, Va., Will Book D–1, 1776–82. VSL.
Hubard Family Papers, 1741–1907. Southern Historical Collection. University of North Carolina Library, Chapel Hill.
[Jefferson, Thomas]. Monticello Music Collection. Alderman Library of the University of Virginia, Charlottesville.
Lee, Philip Ludwell. Manuscript Letter, VHS.
Middlesex County, Va., Will Book B, 1713–34. VSL.
Royle, Joseph. *Virginia Gazette* Daybook. 1764–66. Alderman Library of the University of Virginia, Charlottesville.
Spotsylvania County, Va., Will Book B, 1749–59. VSL.
York County, Va., Wills, Records and Orders, XV. VSL.

B. Printed

Beverley, William. "Diary of William Beverley 'of Blandfield' during a Visit to London in October, 1750," Edited by R. Carter Beverley. *Virginia Magazine of History and Biography* 36: 160–65.
Bolling, Robert. *Memoir of a Portion of the Bolling Family in England and Virginia.* Translated from the French by John Robertson, Jr., Richmond: 1868. Reprint. Berryville, Va.: Chesapeake Book Co. 1964.
Boucher, Jonathan. *Reminiscences of an American Loyalist. 1738–1789.* Edited by Jonathan Bouchier. Boston: Houghton Mifflin, 1925.
Byrd, William. *Another Secret Diary (1739–1741), with Letters and Literary Exercises (1696–1726).* Edited by Maude H. Woodfin. Richmond: Dietz Press, 1942.
——. *The London Diary (1717–1721) and Other Writings.* Edited by Louis B. Wright and Marion Tinling. New York: Oxford University Press, 1958.
——. *The Writings of Col. William Byrd of Westover.* Edited by John Spencer Bassett. New York: Doubleday, Page, 1901.
Carter, Landon. *Diary, 1752–1778.* Edited by Jack P. Greene, 2 vols. Charlottesville: University Press of Virginia for the Virginia Historical Society, 1965.
Cibber, Colley. *An Apology for the Life of Mr. Colley Cibber, Written by Himself.* Edited by Robert W. Lowe. 2 vols. London: John C. Nimmo, 1888. Reprint. New York: AMS Press, 1966.
——. *The Dramatic Works.* 5 vols. London: J. Rivington and Sons, 1777. Facsimile reprint. New York: AMS Press, 1966.
Congreve, William. *Letters and Documents.* Edited by J. C. Hodges. New York: Harcourt, Brace, and World, 1964.
[Dawson, William]. *Poems on Several Occasions.* Reprint. New York: Facsimile Text Society, 1930.
Downes, John. *Roscius Anglicanus.* London: Printed and sold by H. Playford, 1708. Facsimile edition. Los Angeles: University of California Press, Augustan Reprint Society, 1969.
D'Urfey, Thomas. *Wit and Mirth, or Pills to Purge Melancholy.* 4th edn. 6 vols. London: Printed by W. Pearson and J. Tonson, 1719–20. Facsimile of 1876 reprint. New York: Folklore Library Publishers, 1959.
Farquhar, George. *George Farquhar, Four Plays.* Edited by William Archer. New York: Hill and Wang, 1959.
Fielding, Henry. *The Author's Farce.* Edited by Charles B. Woods. Lincoln: University of Nebraska Press, 1966.
Fithian, Philip Vickers. *Journal and Letters.* Edited by Hunter D. Farish. New edn. Williamsburg: Colonial Williamsburg, 1957.
Franklin, Benjamin. *Autobiographical Writings.* Edited by Carl Van Doren. New York: Viking Press, 1945.
——. *The Papers of Benjamin Franklin.* Edited by Leonard W. Labaree. New Haven: Yale University Press, 1968– .
Garrick, David. *Letters.* Edited by David M. Little and George Kahrl. 3 vols. Cambridge: Harvard University Press, 1963.
Goldsmith, Oliver. *Collected Works.* Edited by Arthur Friedman. 5 vols. Oxford: Clarendon Press, 1966.
Grant, Anne. *Memoirs of an American Lady.* New York: Dodd, Meade, 1901.
Harrower, John. *Journal.* Edited by Edward M. Riley. Williamsburg: Colonial Williamsburg, 1963.
Lee, Nathaniel. *Theodosius, or The Force of Love.* London: R. Bentley & M. Magnes, 1680.
The London Stage, 1600–1800. Carbondale: Southern Illinois University Press, 1960—. Pt. I. 1660–1700. Edited by William Van Lennep. 1966. Pt. II. 1700–1729. Edited by Emmett L. Avery. 2 vols. 1960. Pt. III. 1729–1747. Edited by Arthur H. Scouten. 2 vols. 1961. Pt. IV. 1747–1776. Edited by George W. Stone. 3 vols. 1962.
Lower Norfolk County Virginia Antiquary (1895). Edited by Edward W. James. 5 vols. in 2. Reprint. New York: Peter Smith, 1951.
McAleer, John T. *Ballads and Songs Loyal to the Hanoverian Succession, 1703–1761.* Reprint. Los Angeles: University of California Press, 1962.
Muse, Hudson. "Letter of Hudson Muse (Apr. 19, 1771) of Virginia, to his brother, Thomas Muse, of Dorchester County, Maryland." *William and Mary Quarterly* 1st series 2 (1894): 239–241.
O'Hara, Kane. *Midas.* London: T. Lowndes, 6th edn., 1771.
Playbill Collection. Research Department, Colonial Williamsburg.
Shakespeare, William. *A New Variorum Edition of Shakespeare.* 13th edn. Edited by Horace E. Furness. 21 vols. Philadelphia: Lippincott, 1888–1915.
Spence, Joseph. *Anecdotes, Observations, and Characters of Books and Men, as first published from the original Papers with Notes and a Life of the Author by Samuel W. Singer, and now newly introduced by Boramy Dobree.* Carbondale: Southern Illinois University Press, 1964.
Steele, Richard. *Occasional Verse.* Edited by Rae Blanchard. Oxford: Clarendon Press, 1952.
Three Centuries of English Drama. New York: Readex Microprint, 1960.
Washington, George. *Diaries.* Edited by J. C. Fitzpatrick. 4 vols. New York: Houghton-Mifflin, 1925.
——. *The Writings of George Washington from the Original Manuscript Sources, 1745–1799.* Edited by John C. Fitzpatrick. 39 vols. Washington: United States Government Printing Office, 1931–44.
Wood, William. *Personal Recollections of the Stage.* Philadelphia: Henry Carey Baird, 1855.

C. Newspapers and Periodicals

Gentleman's Journal. (London, 1692–94) [HL]
Gentleman's Magazine. (London, 1731–1907)
London Daily Advertiser. (1731–95) [IEAHC microfilm]
London Magazine. (1732–85) [HL]

Maryland Gazette. (1727) [IEAHC]
New York Gazette and Weekly Mercury. (1752–83) [IEAHC]
Pennsylvania Gazette. (1728–1789) (IEAHC]
Pennsylvania Packet. (1771–90) [IEAHC]
The Universal Magazine of Knowledge and Pleasure. (London, 1747–1803) [HL]
Virginia Gazette. (1736–80; see List of Abbreviations for publishers) [CW]

3. SECONDARY SOURCES

ABBOT, WILLIAM A. *A Virginia Chronology*, 1585–1783. Williamsburg: Virginia 350th Anniversary Celebration Corp., 1957.
APPLETON, WILLIAM W. *Charles Macklin: An Actor's Life.* Cambridge: Harvard University Press, 1960.
ASHLEY, LEONARD. *Colley Cibber.* New York: Twayne, 1965.
AVERY, EMMETT L. *Congreve's Plays on the Eighteenth-Century Stage.* New York: Modern Language Association of America, 1951.
BAINE, RODNEY M. *Robert Munford, America's First Comic Dramatist.* Athens: University of Georgia Press, 1967.
BAINES, ANTHONY. *Woodwind Instruments and Their History.* New York: Norton, 1957.
BACKUS, EDYTHE N. *Catalogue of Music in the Huntington Library Printed Before 1801.* San Marino: Huntington Library, 1949.
BALD, ROBERT CECIL. "Sir William Berkeley's Lost Lady." *The Library*, 4th ser. 7 (1937): 395–426.
BARKER, RICHARD. *Mr. Cibber of Drury Lane.* New York: Columbia University Press, 1939.
BELDEN, MARY. *The Dramatic Works of Samuel Foote.* New Haven: Yale University Press, 1929.
BELL, JOHN. *The British Theatre.* 34 vols. London: Printed for John Cawthorne, 1792–98.
BOOTH, MICHAEL R., ed. *Eighteenth-Century Tragedy.* London: Oxford University Press, 1965.
British Union Catalogue of Early Music Printed Before the Year 1801. Edited by Edith B. Schnapper. London: Butterworth Scientific Publications, 1957.
BRONSON, BERTRAND H. *The Traditional Tunes of the Child Ballads.* 2 vols. Princeton: Princeton University Press, 1959.
BROWN, JAMES D. AND STRATTON, STEPHEN S. *British Musical Biography.* London: William Reeves, 1897.
BURNEY, CHARLES. *A General History of Music.* Edited by Frank Mercer. 4 vols. in 2. New York: Dover, 1940.
CARSE, ADAM. *The Orchestra in the Eighteenth-Century.* Cambridge: W. Heffner and Sons, 1940.
CRANE, ROBERT S., ed. *A Collection of English Poems, 1600–1800.* New York: Harper, 1932.
CROSS, WILBUR L. *The History of Henry Fielding.* 3 vols. Reprint. New York: Russell and Russell, 1963.
CHAPPEL, WILLIAM. *The Ballad Literature and Popular Music of the Olden Time.* Edited by Frederick W. Sternfeld. 2 vols. New York: Dover, 1965.
——. *Old English Popular Music.* Edited by H. E. Woolbridge. New York: Brussell, 1961.
CLARK, WILLIAM SMITH. *The Irish Stage in the County Towns, 1720–1800.* Oxford: Clarendon Press, 1965.
CUDWORTH, CHARLES. "Two Georgian Classics: Arne and Stevens." *Music and Letters* 45 (1964): 146–54.
CUSHING, HELEN G. *Children's Song Index.* New York: H. W. Wilson, 1936.
DAVIS, RICHARD BEALE. *George Sandys, Poet-Adventurer.* London: Bodley Head, 1955.
——. *Intellectual Life in Jefferson's Virginia.* Chapel Hill: University of North Carolina Press, 1964.
DAY, CYRUS, AND MURRIE, E. B. *English Song Books, 1650–1702: A Bibliography.* London: Oxford University Press, 1940.
DENT, EDWARD J. *Foundations of English Opera.* New York: Da Capo Press, 1965.
DEUTSCH, OTTO E. *Handel: A Documentary Biography.* New York: Norton, 1954.
Dictionary of American Biography. Edited under the auspices of the American Council of Learned Societies. 22 vols. New York: Scribners, 1928–58.
Dictionary of National Biography. Edited by Leslie Stephen and Sidney Lee. 22 vols. London: Oxford University Press, 1901.
DODSLEY, ROBERT. *A Select Collection of Old English Plays.* 4th edn. Edited by W. Carew Hazlitt. London, 1874–76. Reprint. New York: Blom, 1964.
EDMUNDS, JOHN. *A Williamsburg Songbook.* Williamsburg: Colonial Williamsburg, 1964.
ENGLAND, MARTHA W. *Garrick's Jubilee.* Columbus: Ohio State University Press, 1964.
FINDLAY, ROBERT R. "Macklin's Legitimate Acting Version of *Love a-la-Mode*" *Philological Quarterly* 45 (1966): 749–60.
FISKE, ROGER. "The Macbeth Music," *Music and Letters* 45 (1964): 114–25.
FITZGERALD, PERCY. *Samuel Foote: A Biography.* London: Chatto and Windus, 1910.
FORD, PAUL L. *Washington and the Theatre.* (1899). Reprint. New York: Blom, 1967.
GRAY, CHARLES H. *Theatrical Criticism in London to 1795.* New York: Blom, 1966.
GROVE, SIR GEORGE. *Grove's Dictionary of Music and Musicians.* 3rd edn. Edited by H. C. Colles. 5 vols. and suppl. New York: Macmillan, 1935.
——. *Grove's Dictionary of Music and Musicians.* 5th edn. Edited by Eric Blom. 10 vols. New York: Macmillan, 1954.
H[arrison], F[airfax]. "The Theatre in Eighteenth-Century Virginia, Outside of Williamsburg," *Virginia Magazine of History and Biography* 35 (1927): 295–96.
HARTNOLL, PHYLLIS, ed. *Shakespeare in Music.* New York: Macmillan, 1964.
HAWKINS, SIR JOHN. *A General History of the Science and Practice of Music.* 2 vols. Reprint. New York: Dover, 1963.
HAYWOOD, CHARLES. "William Boyce's 'Solemn Dirge' in Garrick's *Romeo and Juliet* Production of 1750," *Shakespeare Quarterly* 11 (1960): 173–85.
HENDRICK, ROBERT J. *The Lees of Virginia.* New York: Halycon House, 1935.
HILLES, FREDERICK W., ed. *The Age of Johnson.* New Haven: Yale University Press, 1949. Reprint, 1964.
HOWARD, JOHN TASKER. *Music in Washington's Time.* Washington: Washington Bicentennial Commission, 1931.
HUGHES, LEO. *A Century of Farce.* Princeton: Princeton University Press, 1956.
—— and SCOUTEN, A. H., eds. *Ten English Farces.* Austin: University of Texas Press, 1948.
INCHBALD, ELIZABETH, ed. *British Theatre.* 25 vols. London: Longman, Hurst, Rees, and Orme, 1808.
——, ed. *Collection of Farces and Other Afterpieces.* 7 vols. London: Longman, Hurst, Rees, Orme, and Brown, 1815.
IRVING, WILLIAM H. *John Gay, Favourite of the Wits.* New York: Russell and Russell, 1962.
JESTER, ANNIE L., AND HIDEN, M. H., eds. *Adventurers of Purse and Person.* Princeton: Princeton University Press, 1956.

JOHNSON, JAMES. *Scots Musical Museum*, 1787–1803. Notes by W. Stenhouse. Hatboro, Pa.: Folklore Associates, 1962.

KIDD, GEORGE E. *Early Freemasonry in Williamsburg, Virginia.* Richmond: Dietz Press, 1957.

KIMBALL, MARIE. *Jefferson: The Road to Glory, 1743–1776.* New York: Coward, McCann, 1943.

KUNITZ, STANLEY J., AND HAYCRAFT, HOWARD. *British Authors Before 1800.* New York: H. W. Wilson, 1952.

LANGLEY, HUBERT. *Doctor Arne.* Cambridge: Cambridge University Press, 1938.

LEFKOWITZ, MURRAY. *William Lawes.* London: Routledge and Kegan Paul, 1960.

LOEWENBERG, ALFRED. *Annals of Opera*, 1597–1940. 2nd edn., 2 vols. Geneve: Societas Bibliographica, 1955.

LOFTIS, JOHN. *Steele at Drury Lane.* Berkeley: University of California Press, 1952.

LONSDALE, ROGER. *Dr. Charles Burney: A Literary Biography.* Oxford: Clarendon Press, 1965.

MARCUSE, SIBYL. *Musical Instruments: A Comprehensive Dictionary.* Garden City, N.Y.: Doubleday and Co. 1964.

MOLNAR, JOHN W. "A Collection of Music in Colonial Virginia: The Ogle Inventory," *Musical Quarterly* 49 (1963): 150–62.

MOORE, CECIL A., ed. *Twelve Famous Plays of the Restoration and Eighteenth Century.* New York: Modern Library, 1933.

MOORE, ROBERT E. *Henry Purcell and the Restoration Theatre.* Cambridge: Harvard University Press, 1961.

——. "The Music to Macbeth," *Musical Quarterly* 47 (1961): 22–40.

MURRIE, ELEANORE BOSWELL. *The Restoration Court Stage, 1660–1702.* New York: Blom, 1965.

Music Hour, Third Book. New York: Silver Burdett, 1937.

NAGLER, A. M. *A Source Book in Theatrical History.* Reprint. New York: Dover, 1959.

NETTLETON, GEORGE H. *English Drama of the Restoration and Eighteenth Century, 1642–1780.* New York: Macmillan, 1932.

ODELL, GEORGE C. D. *Annals of the New York Stage.* 15 vols. New York: Columbia University Press, 1927.

OMAN, CAROLA. *David Garrick.* Bungay, Suffolk: Hoddert and Staughton, 1958.

O'SULLIVAN, DONAL. *Carolan, the Life, Times, and Music of an Irish Harper.* 2 vols. London: Routledge and Kegan Paul, 1958.

Oxford Companion to Classical Literature. Edited by Sir Paul Harvey. Oxford: Clarendon Press, 1937.

Oxford Companion to English Literature. 3rd edn. Edited by Sir Paul Harvey. Oxford: Clarendon Press, 1945.

Oxford Companion to Music. Edited by Percy A. Scholes. London: Oxford University Press, 1955.

Oxford Companion to the Theatre. Edited by Phyllis Hartnoll. London: Oxford University Press, 1951.

Oxford Dictionary of Nursery Rhymes. Edited by Iona and Peter Opie. London: Oxford University Press, 1951.

PAGE, EUGENE R. *George Colman the Elder.* New York: Columbia University Press, 1935.

PEDICORD, HARRY W. *The Theatrical Public in the Time of Garrick.* Carbondale: Southern Illinois University Press, 1954.

POLLOCK, THOMAS C. *The Philadelphia Theatre in the Eighteenth Century, Together with the Day Book of the Same Period.* Philadelphia: University of Pennsylvania Press, 1933.

PULVER, JEFFREY. *Biographical Dictionary of Old English Music.* New York: E. P. Dutton, 1927.

RANKIN, HUGH F. *The Theater in Colonial America.* Chapel Hill: University of North Carolina Press, 1965.

RENDALL, FRANCIS G. *The Clarinet.* London: Williams and Norgate, 1957.

ROBERTS, EDGAR V. "Mr. Seedo's London Career and his Work with Henry Fielding," *Philological Quarterly* 45 (1966): 179–90.

ROSENFELD, SYBIL M. *Strolling Players and Drama in the Provinces, 1660–1765.* Cambridge: Cambridge University Press, 1939.

——. *Theatre of the London Fairs in the Eighteenth Century.* Cambridge: Cambridge University Press, 1960.

SACHSE, WILLIAM L. *The Colonial American in Britain.* Madison: University of Wisconsin Press, 1956.

SCHOLES, PERCY A. *The Great Doctor Burney.* 2 vols. London: Oxford University Press, 1948.

SEILHAMER, GEORGE O. *The History of the American Theater Before the Revolution.* 3 vols. Philadelphia: Globe Printing House, 1888.

SHAKESPEARE, WILLIAM. *The Complete Works.* Edited by William A. Wright. New York: Garden City Books, 1936.

SHELDON, ESTHER K. *Thomas Sheridan of Smock Alley.* Princeton: Princeton University Press, 1967.

SHUGRUE, MICHAEL, ed. *Regents Restoration Drama Series.* Lincoln: University of Nebraska Press, 1965.

SIMPSON, CLAUDE M. *The British Broadside Ballad and Its Music.* New Brunswick, N.J.: Rutgers University Press, 1966.

SONNECK, OSCAR G. T. *Catalogue of Opera Librettos Printed Before 1800.* Washington: Library of Congress, 1914.

——. *Early Concert Life in America, 1731–1800.* Revised edition. New York: Musurgia Publishers, 1947.

——. *Early Opera in America.* Reprint. New York: Blom, 1963.

——. *Francis Hopkinson and James Lyon.* Reprint. New York: Da Capo Press, 1967.

SOUTHERN, RICHARD. *Changeable Scenery.* London: Faber and Faber, 1952.

SPACKS, PATRICIA ANN. *John Gay, 1685–1732.* New York: Twayne, 1965.

SPENCER, CHRISTOPHER, ed. *Five Restoration Adaptations of Shakespeare.* Urbana: University of Illinois Press, 1965.

STEIN, ELIZABETH P. *Three Garrick Plays.* New York: Blom, 1967.

STOCKWELL, LATOURETTE. *Dublin Theatres and Theatre Customs, 1673–1820.* Kingsport, Tenn.: Kingsport Press, 1938.

TAYLOR, W. D., ed. *Eighteenth-Century Tragedy.* London: Oxford University Press, 1929.

THORP, WILLARD. *Songs from the Restoration Theatre.* Princeton: Princeton University Press, 1934.

THALER, ALWIN. *Shakspere to Sheridan.* Reprint. New York: Blom, 1963.

Thespian Dictionary or Dramatic Biography of the Eighteenth Century. London: T. Hurst, 1802.

TILMOUTH, MICHAEL, ed. *Royal Music Association Research Chronicle No. 1: A Calendar of Reference to Music Published in the Newspapers of London and the Provinces, 1660–1719.* Cambridge: The Royal Music Association, 1961.

U.S. Library of Congress. Jefferson Collection, *Catalogue of the Library of Thomas Jefferson.* Edited by Millicent E. Sowerby. 5 vols. Washington: Library of Congress, 1953–59.

WESTRUP, SIR JACK ALLAN. *Purcell.* New York: Collier Books, 1962.

WILLIS, EOLA. *The Charleston Stage in the Eighteenth Century.* Columbia, S. C.: The State Company, 1924.

WINTON, CALHOUN. *Captain Steele: The Early Career of Richard Steele.* Baltimore: Johns Hopkins Press, 1964.

WRIGHT, RICHARDSON L. *Revels in Jamaica, 1682–1838.* New York: Dodd, Meade, 1937.

ZIMMERMAN, FRANKLIN B. *Henry Purcell: An Analytical Catalogue of His Music.* London: Macmillan, 1963.

——. *Henry Purcell, 1659–1695: His Life and Times.* New York: St. Martin's Press, 1967.

Index

SONGS FROM THE WILLIAMSBURG THEATRE

was designed by Richard Stinely;
set in type, both the text and the music,
by William Clowes and Sons Ltd., London;
lithographed by the Murray Printing Company,
Forge Village, Massachusetts; and
bound by the Kingsport Press, Inc.,
Kingsport, Tennessee.